# A Derrida
# Dictionary

# A Derrida Dictionary

## Niall Lucy

Blackwell
Publishing

350 Main Street, Malden, MA 02148-5020, USA
108 Cowley Road, Oxford OX4 1JF, UK
550 Swanston Street, Carlton, Victoria 3053, Australia

First published 2004 by Blackwell Publishing Ltd

Library of Congress Cataloging-in-Publication Data

Lucy, Niall.
    A Derrida dictionary / Niall Lucy.
        p. cm.
Includes bibliographical references and index.
    ISBN 0-631-21842-4 (alk. paper) – ISBN 0-631-21843-2 (pbk.: alk.
paper)
    1. Derrida, Jacques – Dictionaries.   I. Title.

    B2430 .D483Z865   2004
    194–dc21
                                                    2003012195

A catalogue record for this title is available from the British Library.

Set in 10.5/13pt Minion
by Graphicraft Limited, Hong Kong
Printed and bound in the United Kingdom
by T.J. International Ltd, Padstow, Cornwall

For further information on Blackwell Publishing,
visit our website:http://www.blackwellpublishing.com

In memory of One Tree Hill

# Contents

# Terms

# Abbreviations

See References for full bibliographic details.

| | |
|---|---|
| COO | 'Coming into One's Own' |
| D | *Dissemination* |
| DE | *Deconstruction Engaged* |
| EoT | *Echographies of Television* |
| FoL | 'Force of Law' |
| GoD | *The Gift of Death* |
| GT | *Given Time* |
| LI | *Limited Inc* |
| LJF | 'Letter to a Japanese Friend' |
| MC | 'My Chances' |
| MoP | *Margins of Philosophy* |
| OG | *Of Grammatology* |
| OH | *The Other Heading* |
| ON | *On the Name* |
| OS | *Of Spirit* |
| P | *Positions* |
| PC | *The Post-Card* |
| PoF | *Politics of Friendship* |
| SoM | *Specters of Marx* |
| SP | *Speech and Phenomena* |
| TOJ | 'The Time is Out of Joint' |
| TP | *The Truth in Painting* |
| UG | 'Ulysses Gramophone' |
| VR | 'The Villanova Roundtable' |
| WD | *Writing and Difference* |

Stay, illusion!

*Hamlet*

# Preface

No doubt one could begin by saying all kinds of clever, 'deconstructive' things about why *A Derrida Dictionary* could never be a book of definitions. No doubt, too, one could say some very unclever, undeconstructive kinds of things to begin with, given that many have accused Derrida's 'philosophy' of standing for the impossibility of making positive statements about anything at all. Somewhat ironically, though, both of those beginnings would amount to saying the same thing, which could be summarized as a variation on the opening sentence from Derrida's *Dissemination*:

> This (therefore) will not have been a dictionary.

Hence my aim here has been to provide a series of outlines and interpretations of some of Derrida's key ideas and arguments, rather than a set of fixed definitions. I discuss these (along with the project of deconstruction associated with his name) within the widest context of Continental thought.

I thank Andrew McNeillie and everyone at Blackwell for the support they've shown me throughout. My thanks also to Peta Bowden, Jack Caputo, Steven Connor, John Frow, Kevin Hart, Peggy Kamuf, John Kinsella, Jane Mummery, Chris Norris, Horst Ruthrof, Serge Tampalini, Tony Thwaites and Darren Tofts; and I thank Vijay Mishra, Director of the Krishna Somers Foundation for the Study of Diasporas (Murdoch University), for the chance to present a couple of the entries to a lively group. Above all I am grateful to Rob Briggs and Steve Mickler, whose friendship and critical advice have been constant sources of encouragement.

**aporia**   A Greek term denoting a logical contradiction, 'aporia' is used by Derrida to refer to what he often calls the 'blind spots' of any **metaphysical** argument. The **speech–writing opposition**, for example, could be said to be sustained by an aporia within the opposition 'itself': on the one hand speech can be seen as having to come before writing on the basis only of avoiding that aporia altogether, while on the other the aporia can be shown as necessary to the very constitution of speech and writing as opposites. According to Derrida's deconstruction of the opposition, however, it is writing which comes first. Hence the aporia – or the 'aporetic' moment – takes the form of something that cannot be explained within standard rules of logic: writing can be understood as coming after speech only because in fact it comes before speech. In its most general form, this may be put as follows: **differance** always comes before difference(s).

We should be careful not to see this simply as wilful or 'playful' ingeniousness on Derrida's part. For deconstruction, 'if it is of any consequence', is not reducible to 'a specialized set of discursive procedures' (cited in Culler, *Deconstruction*, 156). While certainly deconstruction is not 'anti-methodological', neither could it be called a 'discourse on method' as such. 'It is also, at the very least', Derrida writes, 'a way of taking a position, in its work of analysis, concerning the political and institutional **structures** that make possible and govern our practices, our competencies, our performances' (ibid.). Note the reference here to the analysis of structures that enable and constrain ('make possible and govern'), which is perhaps a key to understanding deconstruction. What distinguishes a deconstructive analysis, in other words, is that it always begins from an encounter with the aporias that must be overlooked in order to make

ABCDEFGHIJKLMNOPQRSTUVWXYZ

**presence** seem undeconstructible. But if such an encounter is 'deconstructive', this does not preclude it from being philosophical or political at the same time. Indeed, because not only philosophy but also politics depends on the necessity of undeconstructible presence (or presencewithout-difference), then any deconstructive analysis of that dependence – and that logic – could never be anything less than a philosophical and a political analysis as well. (See also DISSEMINATION, GIFT, HYMEN, INSIDE–OUTSIDE, KHORA, *PHARMAKON*, SPECTRALITY, WRITING.)

**artifactuality**    Time does not stand still. What we mean by 'time' today – what it means to be 'in the present' or 'in the here and now' – should not be mistaken for what these might have meant at other times, in other places. Our time today – even what 'today' means today – is made up of features that produce a new concept, or certainly a new experience, of time, albeit one that isn't 'new' in the sense of having come from nowhere, outside of history altogether. In so far as that concept or experience is explicable in terms of the 'made-upness' of time, we can say that time is an artefact. This goes to the heart of what Derrida means by the *artifactuality* of time in the present day.

The point is not that time is artificial, if this defines a pure fiction bearing no relation to actuality or fact. Yet clearly the concept of artifactuality does allude to the *artificiality* of time, but in the sense of 'artifice' understood as **text**. So it is not the absolute fictionality but rather the ineradicable *textuality* of time today that Derrida refers to here. This is to think of the present experience of time – our experience of the present – as something that is produced (made, made up) by what can be called a textual apparatus. Without suggesting that time used to be 'real' before it was made over into 'text', Derrida's argument is that present-day time needs to be understood in terms of modern (or 'postmodern') processes and practices of textualization. It's not possible, in other words, to think of text today without thinking of technology, especially in regards to information and communication. From this it follows that the artifactuality of time and the present refers to the textual production of these concepts by means of contemporary apparatus – what we call 'the media' or, as Derrida often puts it, the whole apparatus of **teletechnology** in general.

To understand what actuality means today we need to look at the ways in which it is *made* in the present, from which we get our sense of 'the present' as such. This necessitates a **responsibility** to analyse the media. 'Hegel was right', Derrida points out, 'to remind the philosopher of his time to read the papers daily. Today, the same responsibility obliges him to learn how the dailies, the weeklies, the television news programs are *made*, and *by whom*' (EoT, 4). But the question of who makes the news isn't reducible to the fact of who owns the means of production. It involves an apparatus of teletechnological processes (which are not simply 'industrial' processes) that no one can 'own'. Take for instance the everyday **event** of a 'live' report on television: 'when a journalist or politician seems to be speaking to us, in our homes, while looking us straight in the eye, he (or she) is in the process of reading, on screen, at the dictation of a "prompter," a text composed somewhere else, at some other time, some-times by others, or even by a whole network of anonymous authors' (ibid.). Such a description of the *making* of actuality on television calls into question the idea that a 'live' bulletin happens only within a moment of **presence** understood as a unique instance of time. Clearly there is a moment at which a live telecast does go out 'live', but the telecast is never reducible to that moment. It is always inscribed in an apparatus of production, making the actual something other than the opposite of the artificial.

It could be said that actuality belongs to the electronic news media today, whose job is to bring the actual into our homes. Every night on our TV screens we are shown footage of things that actually happened some-where in the world that day. In this way actuality on television is inseparable from its teletechnological representation and production, which does not mean the media tell us what to think. The claim instead is that 'the actual' on TV is always an effect of artifactuality, and the target here is not the media but **metaphysics**. To think of actuality in terms of teletechnological production, in other words, is to try to think against an idea of presence, or against the idea that there must be something that guarantees actual events an absolute self-sufficiency, an essence or a meaning all their own, which it is possible to experience in itself or to re-present neutrally. Con-ceived of in terms of presence, the actual must be opposed to the artificial.

Now of course it would be silly to think that Derrida doesn't believe in actuality, because he thinks that actuality is always made up and so every-thing we regard as actual is in fact a complete artifice. The point rather of insisting on the non-opposition of the actual and the artificial has to do with the necessity of opening oneself to the coming of the other, to the radically unforeseeable coming of an event. If we were to see things in terms only of the actual versus the artificial, the factual versus the factitious, we would be closed off to the future. Whenever something was happening, for instance, we would presume to know *that* it was happening and to know *what* it was. In this way actuality would always be given to us in advance – it would always be decided for us in advance – by a sort of programme or **structure**; and this would mean we could never take responsibility for the future. So to oppose the actual to the made is to be closed off to the possibility of what might happen next as something that does not conform to the definition of actuality as given by its opposition to the artificial. That opposition, of course, is the basis of knowledge; what we understand by knowledge requires us to maintain a sharp distinction between the actual and the artificial, the real and the unreal, the living and the dead and so on. It would not count as knowledge, but only as belief, superstition, a form of mysticism, perhaps, to claim there is no difference between those things. Yet our knowledge of the difference between the actual and the artificial is what allows us to construct a 'horizon of expectation', a way of knowing the future in advance. This delimits the status of an event to what actually happens. 'The event cannot be reduced to the fact that something happens. It may rain tonight, it may not rain. This will not be an absolute event, because I know what rain is' (EoT, 13). The meaning of an event, in other words, must be allowed to exceed our *knowledge* of it, based on our acceptance of the opposition of the actual and the artificial.

But there's a danger in this: to call the actual into question is to risk accusations of relativism or revisionism. So any talk of 'artifactuality' could be seen to play into the hands of those who claim the Holocaust didn't happen. By the same token, an uncritical acceptance of the actual as whatever 'is' in its own right, 'outside the text', may lead to all manner of speculative claims about events, about others, about history and so on, ranging from dubious to false. 'What a victory for dogmatisms everywhere', as Derrida puts it, 'if anyone who tries to ask new questions, to upset good consciences or stereotypes, to complicate or reelaborate, in a new situation, the discourse of the left or the analysis of racism and anti-Semitism, stands immediately accused of complicity with the adversary!' (EoT, 16). One thing can always be forced into alignment with another, but clearly there is no necessary connection between artifactuality and Holocaust revisionism. On the contrary, one might say it is all the more necessary to question the concept of actuality in order to oppose revisionism, racism, violence and injustice everywhere. To see the actual only as the undeconstructible opposite of artifice and the artefact is to constrain the 'happening' of the other and of every event; it is to regard others and events as always determinable in advance. This is why it's possible to claim, for instance, that '9/11' (see event) actually means this or that (without question, without fear of contradiction); or to say the threat posed by 'Islam' today is actual. And it makes it possible to say that anyone who would speak out against the actuality of that Islamic threat is a victim of artifice, or is guilty of using artifice to try to deceive 'us'.

Not to question the status of 'fact', or to think one knows with utter certainty what the actual looks like – such conviction underpins all politics. Hence today 'there is a neoprotectionism on the left and a neoprotectionism on the right, in economics as in matters of demographic flux, a free-trade-ism on the right and a free-trade-ism on the left, a neonationalism on the right and a neonationalism on the left' (EoT, 19). What conjoins these opposites – constituting without quite constituting an alliance that is all the more terrifying for being unofficial, unintentional, unconscious – has to do precisely with what Derrida calls the 'permeability' of such concepts as fact and actuality. 'To acknowledge this permeability, this combinatory and its complicities, is not to take an apolitical position' – and it does not mean there is no such thing as 'ideology' or any difference between 'right' and 'left' (ibid.). Instead the purpose is to maintain the radical openness of the future, which is what deconstruction is all about. 'It's better to let the future open – this is the axiom of deconstruction' (ibid.). But as there is no absolute or transcendental warrant that this way is 'better', then to uphold it is to argue for it, to engage in debate over it, to embrace what Derrida calls 'the limitless risk of active interpretation' (EoT, 26). This risk involves the necessity of having to press against the limits of what it means to argue, to debate and to interpret, such that one may stand accused of being relativist, revisionist, apolitical – of having either 'dangerous' arguments or no 'arguments' at all.

Again, the point of insisting on the artifactuality of teletechnological experience today is not to claim that public opinion and political consciousness are controlled by the media. The point is 'to let the future open'. It is to show that what counts as actuality in the present can no longer be confined to the ontological opposition of the actual and the virtual, despite the ongoing necessity of this opposition to every form of politics. Only by pressing at the limits of that opposition is it possible to open a way for thinking differently about others and events. This is to think of them arriving unexpectedly. It is to think of them not in terms of being 'actualized' or becoming 'actual', but as the *arrivant* or **spectre** arrives – at or beyond the limits of arrival, in a time and place which confounds the opposition of the actual and the virtual, life and death and so on, and of everything that draws its existence from the solace of presence. 'The *arrivant*', Derrida writes, 'must be absolutely other, an other that I expect not to be expecting, that I'm not waiting for, whose expectation is made of a nonexpectation, an expectation without what in philosophy is called a horizon of expectation, when a certain knowledge still anticipates and amortizes in advance. If I am sure that there is going to be an event, this will not be an event' (EoT, 13). From this it can be seen that, as a challenge to the ontological opposition of the actual and the virtual, 'artifactuality' does not signify 'the disappearance of the real' under the sway of teletechnological simulacra. Derrida's point in coining the term 'artifactuality' is to emphasize that actuality is 'not given but actively produced, sifted, invested, performatively interpreted by numerous apparatuses which are *factitious* or *artificial*, hierarchizing and selective, always in the service of forces and interests to which "subjects" and agents (producers and consumers of actuality – sometimes they are "philosophers" and always interpreters, too) are never sensitive enough' (EoT, 3).

Such an understanding of the actual as what is always 'actively produced' and 'performatively interpreted' is not an excuse for disengaging from public life or for affecting a disinterest in real-historical events. If the condition of actuality is that it must be made, then it must be able to be made differently (by way of **differance**, for example). That is why it's possible to make another artefact of the other – as the *arrivant*, the absolute stranger. This 'new' ('deconstructive') artefact differs from those available to us now (politically, in the media, in public) by virtue of the lack of a demand for its actuality to be determined in advance, to make itself known to us. While Derrida acknowledges that 'it is practically impossible to think the absence of a horizon of expectation' (EoT, 12), all the same he insists on the necessity of remaining as open as possible to the radical alterity of others. 'I shouldn't ask', he writes, 'the absolute *arrivant* to start by stating his **identity**, by telling me who he is, under what circumstances I am going to offer him hospitality, whether he is going to be integrated or not, whether I am going to be able to "assimilate" him or not in my family, nation, or state' (ibid.).

This does not give others a licence to eat your children, insult your friends or trash your car. It means only that, as a place from which to start, an artefact of the other as *arrivant* leaves open the greatest space for the possibility of a non-violent future to come. (See also DEMOCRACY, GIFT, ITERABILITY, JUSTICE, MESSIANISM, POSTAL METAPHOR, SUPPLEMENT-ARITY, TRACE, UNDECIDABILITY, VIRTUALITY.)

**being** What is the relation of being generally (or Being) to particular beings? This is not a question for cats and dogs, but only for men and women; it's a philosophical and theological question to which there are many possible responses. The one that will concern us here is drawn from **Heidegger** (whose influence on Derrida cannot be overestimated), who would have agreed that the question of Being is for men and women only, though no doubt he would have added that to invoke a concept of 'man' or 'woman' is to get ahead of ourselves. 'First thing you know is that you always have to wait', as the line goes in The Velvet Underground's 'I'm Waiting for the Man' (seeming all of a sudden to be a conspicuously Heideggerean song title).

On Heidegger's account, we need to go back further to a time (which is not historical) before the question of Being was resolved in the form of an essence – man, God, nature and so forth. His project was to try to find a way of understanding Being outside its encapsulation in a concept of subjectivity or consciousness, because any such concept presupposes that our being is located in an 'essence' having the quality of a 'thing'. Instead of 'man' or 'subject', then, Heidegger uses the term *Dasein* ('being-there' or strictly 'there-being') to refer to the form of being that is capable of asking the question of Being. 'What is Being?' is not a question asked by literature, dolphins or rocks (each of which is a form of being); it is a question that only *Dasein* asks. Hence the capacity to ask the question of Being is a distinctive feature of *Dasein*'s being, of that form of being-in-particular.

This brings us to the ontico-ontological difference, the difference between beings and Being. The distinction has to do with needing to separate an 'ontic' world of particular things (particular beings, for example) from the 'ontological' question of how it might be possible to have an experience of such things. In a sense, *Dasein*'s philosophy has always posed the question of Being ontically; it has asked the question of this or that particular form of being. Heidegger insists, however (in *Being and Time*), that our world is *ontological* – it is not reducible simply to what is there before us in the present but exists rather as the possibility of things coming to **presence**. It is this ontological dimension that allows us to say of any thing, 'there is' (*es gibt*); and so according to this ontological understanding of the world, the world allows – as a sort of **gift** (*es gibt* translates also as 'it gives') – things to come 'to be'.

The gift of Being is being-in-the-world, meaning that *Dasein*'s being is given in its relations (or relatedness) to everything that 'is' in the world. This is to conceive of the world (to understand it ontologically) as a totality not simply of things, but also languages, historical trajectories, social movements, political agendas – and, of course, other people. *Dasein*'s being is given, then, in its relations with the world as a totality of others: the relatedness of 'being there' to 'being with'. To forget or to fail to see the necessity of this relatedness would be to miss something 'authentic' and essential to *Dasein*; it would be to look at something only ontically (to see a problem or a concept, for instance, as a thing) and therefore to miss seeing the 'worldliness' of the world. By the same token it should be noted that Heidegger did not really think there was a way out of the ontico-ontological difference, as though it might be possible to find a way back past **metaphysics** to the **origin** of Being or thought. This is so because although the ontological dimension of Being has been forgotten by metaphysics, nevertheless the very question of Being as such is inseparable from what *Dasein* 'is' – in which case it is not only ontological but also ontic. So for Heidegger there is no question of returning to a time that was *purely* ontological, a place outside of metaphysics altogether.

Yet this could be to succumb to a sort of obligatory pressure to say that Heidegger was not searching for the lost origin of Being, and in Derrida's view that may not be quite the right thing to say. So for all that Heidegger's influence on Derrida cannot be overestimated, neither should the differences between them be overlooked – especially when it comes to politics. 'Derrida is as far removed from Heidegger on this matter of politics', John D. Caputo writes, to great comic effect, 'as a Parisian, post-Marxist left intellectual can be from a right-wing, reactionary, mountain-climbing anti-Marxist and anti-modernist' (*Nutshell*, 153). Take for instance Derrida's reflections on Heidegger's reading of the Anaximander fragment (in *Early Greek Thinking*), where Heidegger associates **justice** (*dike*) with jointure, harmony and accord, and injustice (*adikia*) with being 'out of joint' (see SoM, 23–4).

The present (according to the Anaximander fragment) is unhinged or out of joint (*adikia*), which Derrida says Heidegger takes to mean that something must have gone missing, something must have been lost already – by the time of the early Greeks. Why? Because, Heidegger asks, how could the present (any present, or the presence of the present) be out of joint? Out of joint with what, for instance? Compared to when? This is not to say that Heidegger reads the relation of *dike* to *adikia* in terms of a succession: first there is *dike*, then there is *adikia*. But he does skew the difference between them '*in favour* of what he in effect interprets as the possibility of *favour* itself, of the accorded favour, namely, of the accord that gathers or collects while harmonizing' (SoM, 27). On the one hand *dike* is the gift of justice – it is given to Being, it is '**proper**' to Being and it gives Being presence (SoM, 26–7). So to do justice is to give to others what is theirs already, the accord within Being. But on the other hand Heidegger knows that disjointure (*adikia*) is within presence, too. The presence of the present, then, is simply what 'lingers awhile' in the in-between space or passage of 'what leaves and what arrives, at the articulation between what absents itself and what presents itself' (SoM, 25). Yet to the extent that *dike* and *adikia* are opposed to one another (in Heidegger's reading) they cannot lead to Derrida's radical sense of the other's absolute **undecidability** or the absolute incalculability of justice. To say that *dike* 'is' justice, that the accord is *proper* to being (with or without a capital 'B'), is to presume to know in advance what justice and being mean. If *dike* 'is' justice, then justice is determinable; hence it reduces to 'the law'. And if there *is* something that is proper to being, doesn't this return being to subjectivity?

In order to let others be, being cannot be understood as presence. For others to be allowed to be radically, absolutely and unknowably other, I must not think of them as beings. Or at least I must think of them as beings without being – all the dis-joined, dis-adjusted, dis-possessed others who are here now, who have gone and are yet to come, but who are not gathered together (as a nation, a community, a species) in any kind of harmonious accord, and especially not the Grand Accord of Being. Any such gathering presumes that every different other is 'appropriable as the same' (SoM, 27). In order to think being otherwise, however, others must be allowed to come unexpectedly, to whom justice must be given in excess of what is owed. (See also DEMOCRACY, EVENT, IDENTITY, RESPONSIBILITY, SPECTRALITY, SUPPLEMENTARITY.)

**chora**  See *khora*.

**deconstruction** If I paint a milk bottle red, I won't have 'deconstructed' it. If I wear nail polish, I won't have 'deconstructed' my sexuality. If I vote conservative in protest at the failures of the parliamentary left, I won't have 'deconstructed' politics.

Whatever deconstruction is (if it 'is' at all), it is not reducible to an attitude of nonconformity, oppositionality or principled resistance. Indeed the list of what deconstruction is not can be made to go on more or less indefinitely. Deconstruction is not, for instance, a form of critique, either 'in a general sense or in a **Kantian** sense' (LJF, 273); it is not a method or a theory; it is not a discourse or an operation. This is not intended to avoid making positive statements about deconstruction for the sake of making it seem that deconstruction is impossibly difficult to define. While in a sense it is impossibly difficult to define, the impossibility has less to do with the adoption of a position or the assertion of a choice on deconstruction's part than with the impossibility of every 'is' as such. Deconstruction begins, as it were, from a refusal of the authority or determining power of every 'is', or simply from a refusal of authority in general. While such refusal may indeed count as a position, it is not the case that deconstruction holds this as a sort of 'preference'. It's not that deconstruction prefers or chooses to deconstruct the **presence** of a thing, as though it could choose to prefer to see things as being undeconstructible. Deconstruction is not a 'method' that can be 'applied' to something with a view to deconstructing it. If things are deconstructible, they are deconstructible already – as things. Or as Derrida puts it in one of many approximations of a definition of deconstruction, to say that deconstruction consists of anything would be to say it consists of 'deconstructing, dislocating, displacing, disarticulating, disjoining, putting "out of joint" the authority of the "is" ' (TOJ, 25). Contrary to an earlier remark, then, we could say perhaps that it *would* be deconstructive to paint a milk bottle red, since this might help to show the non-essentialness of what a milk bottle 'is': it is not essential that a milk bottle should be colourless, in other words. Showing this might help to open or unsettle the seeming imperviousness of a concept of essence or **identity** in general, concerning fixed ideas of politics, **being**, truth and so on. But if we can use the example of painting a milk bottle red as an example of deconstruction, then surely we would have to concede (as Derrida indicates in the 'Letter to a Japanese Friend') that deconstruction is everything and nothing at the same time. 'All sentences of the type "deconstruction is X" or "deconstruction is not X" *a priori* miss the point', Derrida writes, because deconstruction is not reducible to an essential feature, task or style (LJF, 275). We could not even say that what is essential to deconstruction is its 'non-positivity' or 'non-essentialness'. Like every word (and the same could be said for every thing) deconstruction 'acquires its value from its inscription in a chain of possible substitutions' (ibid.). Always within a context, that is to say, the word *deconstruction* 'replaces and lets itself be determined by such other words' as **differance**, *pharmakon*, **trace**, **supplement**, **hymen**, **iterability**, *parergon* and the like (ibid.). But again there is nothing that could be said to be essential to deconstruction in its differential relations with other words. For this to be the case would mean that every word *is* what the dictionary defines it to be, as though somehow every definition could be taken as meaningful on its own.

To put it tentatively, deconstruction might be said to be what 'happens' to things. 'Deconstruction takes place,' Derrida writes, 'it is an **event** that does not await the deliberation, consciousness, or organization of a subject, or even of modernity. *It deconstructs it-self. It can be deconstructed [Ça se déconstruit]*' (LJF, 274). This is why we cannot afford to think of deconstruction as a general theory or method of reading, say, or interpretation, which can be brought from somewhere 'outside' a **text**, a theme, an object or a problem and applied to the 'inside' of that thing. Deconstruction is precisely what helps us to see (and of course also to say) that **inside–outside** relations are always already 'in' deconstruction. In a sense, this means that deconstruction doesn't help us to see or to say anything 'new', in so far as deconstruction is not a cause of the deconstructibility of a binary opposition or the relation of any inside to an outside and so on. But of course once it is accepted that every binary opposition, for example, is already in deconstruction, there can be no going back to a way of understanding that requires the terms of any binary pair to be seen according to an absolute and a priori difference. 'One of the two terms governs the other (axiologically, logically, etc.), or has the upper hand', Derrida writes in reference to the terms of any classical or binary opposition (P, 41), and so in this respect the opposition is never of the order of a neutral difference but always of 'a violent hierarchy' (ibid.). What might be called the work of deconstruction, then, involves the necessity of a double movement, which is irreducible to a 'two-step programme' or successive 'phases' of interpretation. Once again, deconstruction is not something that is brought *to* an opposition; it is the impossible condition of possibility of every opposition, whether it be man–woman, **speech–writing**, inside–outside, etc. Hence the 'double movement' (or **writing**) of deconstruction involves both an inversion of the hierarchical relationship on whose occlusion or suppression the 'neutrality' of the difference between the terms of any binary pair depends, *and* the 'irruptive emergence of a new "concept"', as Derrida puts it, which is not really a 'concept' at all inasmuch as the very concept of a concept depends on an idea of difference-as-presence, allowing one to say of something that 'it' is. 'By means of this double, and precisely stratified, dislodged and dislodging, writing, we must also mark the interval between inversion, which brings low what was high, and the irruptive emergence of a new "concept," a concept that can no longer be, and never could be, included in the previous regime' (P, 42). It is important to repeat that Derrida is not referring here to something that deconstruction 'does' to oppositions, but rather to what *happens* to oppositions in and as 'themselves'. In the case of the speech–writing opposition, for instance, Derrida shows that writing comes before speech, thus inverting the standard hierarchy. What the opposition depends on, then, is the oppression of writing's originariness. But of course once you accept that writing comes before speech, you can no longer think of 'writing' in terms of the conceptual limits that are ascribed to it from within the **structure** of an opposition. You have to try to think of a new 'concept' of writing, even if it could never quite be a concept as such according to the terms of 'the previous regime'. Yet again the point is that this new concept (which would not *be* a concept) would not be something that was 'new' in the sense of being unprecedented or original. It would 'be there' already; it would have been happening already. 'I have often had occasion to define deconstruction', Derrida has said recently, 'as that which is – far from a theory, a school, a method, even a discourse, still less a technique that can be appropriated – at bottom *what happens or comes to pass*' (TOJ, 17). Like it or not, in other words, deconstruction is a happening thing! (See also APORIA, DISSEMINATION, LOGOCENTRISM, METAPHYSICS, ORIGIN, PHONOCENTRISM.)

**democracy**    Australia is a democratic nation in which the right to vote is also an obligation, a legally enforceable one: failure to vote incurs a fine and carries the risk of a prison sentence. In Australia the right to vote is interpreted literally, as it were, or in purely positivist terms – it does not extend to a citizen's democratic right to choose not to vote. Choosing not to vote is not a voting option in Australia, but is seen only as the avoidance of one's political duty and not as the conscious expression of a citizen's political intention or volition.

What is a right that is also an obligation, a duty bound by law? We might be able to see the sense in punishing someone for infringing the rights of another, but by what logic could someone be punished for not exercising a right that 'belongs' to him or her and which surely ought to include the right not to exercise that right? These questions take us to the limits of democracy as the name of a political system that enshrines a notion of the rights of citizens to free association, free expression, free passage and so on. Paradoxically, however, such democratic freedoms are never absolute: the right to free association does not include the right to form a racist militia; freedom of expression does not allow you to give vent to religious vilification; free passage extends only to the law-abiding citizens of a nation and not to others who may wish to become citizens of that nation but who 'fall' outside the immigration laws. In every democracy, then, rights and rules go together – and there is a sense in which this always compromises the idea or the ideal of democracy as a social contract that guarantees rights, freedom and equality to everyone. But of course by 'everyone' is not meant people in general, all the people of the world, but only the lawful citizens of this or that democratic nation, and even then usually only those citizens who conform to an idea of normal subjectivity. Every democracy, then, is also a nation, even though we might say that the idea of democracy passes beyond all national borders.

As an idea, democracy is irreducible to the practices of any parliamentary system or the representative politics of any nation state. It is even irreducible today, as Derrida argues, to an idea of parliament or parliamentary representation as such, given that the public sphere in which relations between citizens and their elected representatives are conducted (according to an 'old' political model) has been reconfigured by 'techno-tele-media apparatuses and by new rhythms of information and communication' (SoM, 79). This transformation of the public sphere into what is sometimes called the mediascape requires politicians to act as other than professional parliamentarians, or else risk becoming '*structurally* incompetent' regardless of any competence they might have as elected advocates in a strict or old-fashioned sense (SoM, 80). The increasing televisualization and technologization, moreover, of public space has led to the production of new concepts of **event** and fact. The obvious case in point is the spectre – the **spectral** effect – of Osama bin Laden, whose phantom-like existence is a pure media *event* made up out of rumours, accusations and videotape. From within this construction is projected the fact of his existence 'outside the **text**' in a cave somewhere in the Middle East, the exact location of which continues (as I write) to befuddle all the techno-military and economic resources of the world's last remaining superpower in attempts to uncover it. If such an event, if such a fact or set of facts, were not truly real, it would make for a truly implausible story.

Yet even if Osama bin Laden were ever to be found (dead or alive), he could never be found outside the text, or outside the particular textualization of his 'evil' politics, 'religious' zealotry and 'xenophobic' hatred of the West. This is not intended to exonerate bin Laden of the charges that have been levelled at him, or to condone acts of violence and sabotage as exemplified by what has come to be known as '9/11'. It is intended rather to acknowledge that whatever 'Osama bin Laden' is agreed to signify (or for that matter 'Saddam Hussein', 'Muslim extremists', 'terrorist cabals', etc.) has not been decided on the floors of parliamentary democracies by elected representatives engaged in vigorous debates conducted on Enlightenment principles of tolerance and reason in the search for truth. Wherever the significations have come from (the point is that their locations are irreducible to geo-temporal or phenomenological coordinates, and irreducible as well to conspiratorial intent), their effectivity puts 'in question electoral democracy and political representation *such at least as we have known them up until now*' (SoM, 79). Again, this is not to invoke the spectre of a media conspiracy, or of a conspiratorial alliance of the media and the military, in the production of what used to be called ideological truth or simply ideology. As a certain mode of signification or textuality of the other, nevertheless, 'Osama bin Laden' is an exemplary instance of one-dimensional man or, as E. M. Forster might have put it, a sort of 'flat' character (see Forster, *Aspects*). In this his textuality differs markedly from that of the most monstrous figures in literature – Lady Macbeth, Captain Ahab, Milton's Satan and the like – all of whom are writ large in terms of the complexity of their moral and psychic interiors and their socio-political reckonings, which opens the way for imaginative possibilities concerning the sorts of decisions and judgements that might be formed in relation to them. Literature is not of course the only medium, or the only kind of **writing**, that could be said to open the possibility of 'free passage' between selves and others. But certainly as a particular instance of textual 'free expression' (perhaps even of 'free trade'), literature is on side with democracy in terms of expanding possibilities for thought and imagination, including (if not especially) the possibility of what it may be impossible to think or imagine. This could be literature's **gift**, its own particular form of an 'experience of the impossible' (FoL, 15) or the 'ordeal' of **undecidability** (FoL, 24), which is no doubt why Derrida never poses the difference between literature and philosophy in terms of a choice between 'writing' and 'thinking'.

Such a choice could be based only on the presumption that differences between texts, or between 'genres' of textuality, conform to 'essential' differences as marked out in the periodic table of the elements. According to this **metaphysics** or **logocentrism**, textual differences are equivalent to natural differences. So any choice between literature and philosophy, say, would have to proceed from the idea that, at base, each is as different from the other as hydrogen is from zinc. Differences conceived of in this fashion are effects of **presence**, making the differences between texts in culture as secure as the differences between elements in nature.

One does not think of hydrogen in terms of heterogeneity, an open future or an ongoing process of becoming: its unmistakable **identity** depends on the acceptance of its having come into the world (or come to presence) already, prior to any discovery of it. Chemists and physicists could not work with hydrogen if they believed that its elemental 'identity' remains always to come, forever inscribed in the **iterability** of its own perpetually altering formation. Without the periodic table of the elements, in other words, there could be no chemistry or physics. But the more pressing point here is that, without a conceptual equivalent of the periodic table of the elements, there could be no metaphysics.

'Who's there?' is not a question we would ever ask of hydrogen. But it is the question that Barnardo asks at the very beginning of Shakespeare's *Hamlet*, and we might say that this question, which opens the play, remains open still at the end. In *Hamlet* the question of who or what is there cannot be decided on the basis of a periodic table of differences. Who is there, for example, in the figure of Hamlet himself – a madman, a righteous avenger, a jealous son, etc.? Who's there in his mother's bed, and who is she as a consequence? Who's there in the Prince of Denmark that he could have been responsible for Ophelia's death? Who's there in Polonius, who blows with the wind? And of course who or what is there in the 'thing' that appears onstage in the likeness of the dead King, having been 'twice seen' already, before the play begins, posing the question of *when* the play begins?

Questions of identity and temporality (who? when?) permeate Shakespeare's play. But in Derrida's reading of *Hamlet* (in *Specters of Marx*) they are not reducible to themes. The ghost in *Hamlet* could be said to pose the questions *Who am I? When am I?* (What is my **being**? What is my time?). But for Derrida these cannot be confined to effects upon the characters and events in that text 'itself', as if *Hamlet* were a self-contained or self-sufficient entity in a periodic table of fully constituted textual differences. They extend rather to questions of being and time in general. And as such they are not simply literary or aesthetic questions that we might choose to puzzle over at our leisure or according to some privilege. On Derrida's argument they are urgently political questions that call for a response in the absence of any programme, preconceived agenda or 'periodic table' of appropriate actions. If it were a matter simply of having to comply with a programme or to fulfil a duty, then in very quick succession Hamlet would remonstrate with his mother, execute Claudius, marry Ophelia and assume the throne – all before the end of Act Two. What prevents this from happening is precisely that Hamlet cannot answer the question, *Who's there?* And he cannot do so because the question is unanswerable, even though it demands a response. From the moment that Hamlet has an 'experience of the impossible' in his encounter with the ghost, the question of who or what is there – the question even of what *there* means ('The time is out of joint') – calls and keeps on calling to him. What makes him go 'mad' is not knowing how to respond to that question; all he knows is that he cannot not respond. He cannot (as it were) choose not to vote.

That at least would not be a sufficient or satisfying response, any more than it would be sufficient or satisfying for Hamlet to act simply out of a sense of duty. Doing one's duty does not entail having to make decisions, which must always risk being wrong. To perform a duty is to follow a prescriptive course of action, or to complete a transaction from within an economy or circle of exchange. It is to undertake an obligation to give to the other only what the other is owed, which might be a card on Father's

Day or a grade without comments on a student essay. Inside the economic circle, then, time is seemingly never out of joint and there is no hope of asking, *Who's there?* Defined as a set of economic transactions, social relations can be understood in terms only of obligation, and this might explain the legislative logic by which Australia (though it's not alone in this respect) has transformed the right to vote into a compulsion to vote.

In its official conception at any rate the Australian demos is less than democratic. But this doesn't mean that, by contrast, there are other nations that are somehow 'fully' democratic, because the whole point of democracy as an ideal is that it cannot arrive at plenitude or come to presence. (In a sense, democracy is **postal**.) As an ideal, democracy calls us to conceive of social relations in terms of **responsibility** rather than of obligation, which rules out any hope of responding to others by reference to a periodic table of social or moral prescriptions. In responding to others, 'rules' are what we have to make up as we go along. This is to acknowledge that social responsibility calls for a degree of creative or inventive work on the part of social beings, since the indeterminate nature of responsibility renders it impossible to fulfil. 'One is never responsible enough', as Derrida puts it (GoD, 51). Yet what we might call the 'experience of the impossible' that responsibility brings us to is not something that only philosophy can teach us. It is also, Derrida argues, part of every social being's daily life. In his own case, for example, Derrida may be said to fulfil his 'duty', as a philosopher and a citizen, whenever he speaks or writes 'in a public language', which of course for him is French (GoD, 69). But at the same time he acknowledges (or confesses) that by undertaking to fulfil those obligations he is also 'sacrificing and betraying at every moment all my other obligations: my obligations to the other others whom I know or don't know' (ibid.). We can't allow responsibility to be defined, then, simply as public or professional accountability. To leave responsibility at that would be to suppose that everyone has assigned to them a certain *quantum* of responsibility to fulfil. And responsibility cannot be quantified. It is never enough for someone to be accountable as a citizen or a professional, or in any other 'role' (as father, Christian, Marxist, patriot or friend and so on). In this way, by undertaking to fulfil his responsibilities as a public intellectual, Derrida is forced (as we all are) to 'betray' an ideal of responsibility, or what we might call responsibility in general, whose demands are impossibly overwhelming. To be responsible as a citizen or a professional philosopher is also to be irresponsible (not responsible 'enough') at the same time. Responsibility necessitates irresponsibility. In Derrida's case this means that in order to be a good citizen or a philosopher he has to betray what it might otherwise be possible 'to be', beyond the limits of being-in-public, for example, or beyond those pertaining to a concept of citizenship or an idea of professionalism. Hence he concedes that, by fulfilling his public and professional duty, 'I betray my fidelity or my obligations to other citizens, to those who don't speak my language and to whom I neither speak nor respond, to each of those who listen or read, and to whom I neither respond nor address myself in the **proper** manner, that is, in a singular manner' (GoD, 69).

Derrida often couches singularity (which for him is tied, as can be seen from the passage above, to responsibility) in terms of secrecy. The nature of any secret is such that it must always remain unpresentable. For a secret 'to be' what 'it is', it cannot be brought into language (whether that of a nation or a profession) or be made public. A secret always keeps itself to itself, keeps quiet about itself, refusing to give up its singularity or to let itself be translated into any idiom conceived of as determinable (positive *or* negative). While it's possible to tell a secret, it is not possible to tell *secrecy* as such: the secrecy of every secret is always unpresentable. For this reason Derrida sees an affinity between secrecy and 'the sacred' (GoD, 21), where the latter might be said to stand for an 'experience of the impossible' that takes us outside of ourselves but which can't be put into words or be located within consciousness, or in terms of any determinable choice between what 'is' and 'is not'. (And certainly it could not be found according to the rules and practices of any religious or other institution.) As an 'experience of the impossible', the sacred cannot be institutionalized or translated. To attempt to do so would be to deny its singularity, as though whatever the sacred 'is' should be made accountable to a language we know and use already – the one (whether of a nation or a profession) we are accustomed to speaking and writing *in public*. In terms of the relations between secrecy, singularity and the sacred, then, we can say that there is never any answer to the question, *Who's there?* To demand an answer to it would be to make others accountable to 'us', to what is familiar to us, in terms of our language, our ways of making sense, our laws and customs. This would be to impose on others the responsibility to translate *their* unpresentability – their sacred and secret singularity – into the metaphysics of presence. It is just as inhospitable to attempt to detain others within metaphysics as it is to detain refugees within prison-like 'centres' while they await 'our' decision in answer to the question, *Who's there?*

The problem though is that both forms of detention go together, such that a deep affinity inheres between barbed words and barbed wire – so deep as to constitute a sort of secret history. While that affinity knows no respect for national borders, cultural identities or political organizations, nevertheless it only ever belongs officially (from 'our' point of view) to someone else's past, as something that marks *their* being in the present and for the future. Yet if the affinity between metaphysical and physical detention is foreign to democracy as an ideal (democracy in general), it would be a mistake to suppose that it has never had a place in the history of democracies in particular. To make that mistake would be to fail to ask the question of every democratic nation's responsibility *today* for what Derrida chose to 'sum up', in 1994 or thereabouts, 'with an ellipsis in the expression "appropriation of Jerusalem"' (SoM, 59). For what is happening today in and around the place and the figure of 'the Middle East' cannot be understood as a physical or even a political confrontation only, or as an 'event' as it used to be known. Gathered there (but where?) today are 'all the forces of the world and the whole "world order"', taking such disparate forms as 'the old concepts of State and nation-State, of international law, of tele-techno-medio-economic and scientifico-military forces, in other words, the most archaic and the most modern spectral forces' (ibid.). To suppose that the question of democracy comes down to a difference between voting as a right or an obligation would be to mistake democracy as an ideal for its always less than ideal phenomenological, historical, political or public manifestations. Whatever democracy 'is' must include the possibility of what it might remain 'to come', which must include the possibility of an indeterminate future that cannot be predicted on the basis of a knowledge and experience of the present understood in terms of the past.

This is why Derrida conceptualizes democracy (by another logic, as it were) in terms of what always remains *to come*. 'Far from effacing differences and analytic determinations', he writes, 'this other logic calls for other concepts' (SoM, 163). Among these, as we've seen, are included 'new' concepts of event and fact, as well as those concerning politics and the public, whose 'old' formations are derived from an Enlightenment faith in the rational subject's critical powers of observation and analysis. Such faith was entwined, of course, with a belief in reasonableness, and it is to this conjunction that we owe our modern concept of democracy. But this is not to say that henceforth we should abandon all assurance in the Enlightenment, now that the global event of the 'war on terror', for example, cannot be explained as an event according to an Enlightenment understanding of that concept. If it can be said that we get our ideas regarding rights, independence, justice and democracy, and the like, from the Enlightenment, then who in his right mind would want to come out today against the Enlightenment and the promise it represents? Derrida's problem with the Enlightenment, if he has one, is not that its democratic promise of a better future may be criticized for being masculinist or Eurocentric (which is not to say it can't be), but that the promise is founded on an uncritical acceptance of the self-present rationality of the sovereign subject. To the extent that this acceptance is uncritical (a foundational article of Enlightenment faith), then it is also anti-Enlightenment. Hence for **deconstruction** to be critical of such assent (in so far as deconstruction can be called a critique of the metaphysics of presence) would mean it could never be opposed to the Enlightenment, which taught us to value being critical – and also to value rights, independence, justice, democracy and the like. But it taught us those values from within metaphysics, which is why Derrida argues that we need to rethink our ideas about such things as rights and democracy if we no longer believe in the undeconstructability of the rational subject.

If none of us is an autonomous, self-sufficient, self-present, fully different-entiated, conscious, intentional, rational being, then we need to be very careful about how we respond (for ourselves and on behalf of others) to the question, *Who's there?* If the least we can say about each of us is that every one of us is a social being, then the only response to that question is to say, *Come hither.* This of course is not how the citizens of any nation have ever responded to that question, and that is why democracy must always be allowed to remain *to come*, regardless of national interests and politics. Again, the radical idea of a democracy to come is not anti-Enlightenment, but certainly Derrida does intend it to exceed the conceptual and public limits of Enlightenment concepts of citizenship, parliamentary representation and the nation state, which rely on coastguards and border patrols to police those limits and to tell us all who's there. The 'new' concept of a democracy to come (which is also a radical extension of the Enlightenment concept of democracy and therefore not 'new' in any absolute or original sense) could never belong to any national political-administrative system, but only to each and every one of us as members of a spectral community. The 'citizens' of a democracy to come (which is what democracy has always been and must always be) could never be conjoined under a constitution, a set of public laws or a party-political system. Their sense of identity – their spectrality – would be of an order invoked by the title of one of Funkadelic's best-known songs, 'One Nation under a Groove'. Since a 'groove' cannot be objectified, quantified or calculated, yet isn't totally unreal or imaginary either, we can say it is spectral. But it doesn't follow from this that deconstruction has nothing to do with body politics, as if all it had to offer were some kind of out-of-body experience of the political by calling us to forswear thinking for dancing. To try to imagine a nation under a 'groove', rather than under a government or a constitution, would be to try to think of nationhood differently, as something other than a self-proclaimed territory with the self-appointed 'right' to ward off 'intruders'. A nation under a groove could never take the form of a nation state; as a concept of nationhood, then, it could be said to be post-Enlightenment. What would a nation be that was not a nation state?

That question is attributable not only to Funkadelic, or at any rate to George Clinton who wrote the song. For, long before the release (in 1978) of 'One Nation under a Groove', Marx implored us to imagine a certain concept of 'nations without nationalism', to borrow a term of Julia Kristeva's (see Kristeva, *Nations*), in the spectral figure of an international alliance of workers. This would be an organized 'citizenry' of labour united under its oppression by capitalism. Marx's promise of an actual future to come, of a world in which power and wealth would be redistributed according to notions of equality and equity, has not yet been realized, but it is precisely the promisory and not the predictive power of his political projection that is the measure of its democratic force. Today, now that Marx and Marxism are dead and supposedly buried, it is said publicly that democracy is threatened by the terrifying spectre of 'the Middle East' whose monstrous unifying power is the miscreant issue of anti-Christian intolerance and anti-Western resentment belonging to a pre-Enlightenment way of life. And so today we live in fear of a bio-chemical terror to come, in a tomorrow just around the corner when the pre-modern Middle East unleashes its postmodern weapons of mass destruction upon all the freethinking, free-trading, freedom-loving peoples of the democratic West. Having exorcized the spectre of communism, democracy must now ward off the sinister intentions and phantasmagoric powers of ancient Islam.

This is not meant to suggest that Islamic nationalism is akin to Marx's conception of an international (or transnational) alliance of citizen-workers, or that the present-day regime in Iraq, for instance, is something that the concept of democracy-to-come should embrace. The point rather is that the 'war on terror' is irreducible to the formula, *democratic freedom versus anti-democratic ideology*. This is because the concept of democracy (or the 'new' concept of democracy-to-come) exceeds the limits of conceptualization as given to us from within the metaphysics of presence, where it's possible to think that 'democracy' means a particular system of government and in turn that other systems must as a result be called 'anti-democratic'. Of course this is true, but as an explanation of what democracy means it is also not enough. For Derrida's radical concept of democracy-to-come would always be 'out of joint' with that explanation; certainly it would be out of joint with time or history, for example, understood in terms of presence – as the past-present behind the present day that opens onto the present of tomorrow. Indeed the very **teletechnological** constitution of experience in the present day 'obliges us more than ever to think the virtualization of space and time, the possibility of virtual events whose movement and speed prohibit us more than ever (more and otherwise than ever, for this is not absolutely and thoroughly new) from opposing presence to its representation, "real time" to "deferred time", effectivity to its simulacrum' (SoM, 169). It is from here (but where?), beyond the opposition of the real and the virtual, the living and the dead and so on, that we must think differently today about what a place means – 'the places of lovers, families, nations' (ibid.) – in order that we might go on thinking about what it means to live, 'but without killing the future in the name of old frontiers' (ibid.). Nations that act only in the interests of nationalism (whether they are called, or call themselves, a democratic republic, a communist state or an Islamic regime) 'not only sow hatred, not only commit crimes, they have no future, they promise nothing even if, like stupidity or the unconscious, they hold fast to life' (ibid.). In such a context there could be no more pressing responsibility today than to think 'another space for democracy. For democracy-to-come and thus for justice' (ibid.). For Derrida, the space for that democracy – for democracy that says, *Come hither* – is opened by the spectre, the one who says, 'Remember me!'

What can it mean to 'remember' a ghost? This question is puzzling only from within a space of thinking 'controlled or fixed by the simple opposition of presence and absence, actuality and inactuality, sensuous and supersensible', etc. (SoM, 163). For in truth, as a possibility or an expectation, the ghost is always already there, and so it can and must be remembered even if it poses the difficulty of what it means to 'remember' something, or someone, that is never and has never been not present. As Derrida writes of the ghost in *Hamlet*, 'the ghost is there, be it in the opening of the promise or the expectation, *before its first apparition*' (ibid.). And this im-possible temporality, aligned with the im-possibility of the ghost's being there, obliges us to 'think otherwise the "time" or the date of an event. Again: "ha's this thing appear'd againe tonight?"' (ibid.).

The exemplary instance of an historical date today is '9/11'. However, to suppose that what happened on that day did not happen for the first time (in the sense of being utterly original, the very thing in itself) would not mean having to deny that thousands of people did actually die in Manhattan on 11 September 2001 and that millions of others around the world were stricken with fear and loathing as they watched it happening over and over again on television. But what exactly were we watching? To say the very least, 9/11 is still open to conjecture. Whatever happened on that day did not happen within time understood as presence, and whatever happened 'then' continues to happen 'now'. So already 9/11 has stretched forward, well beyond the date itself, and no doubt will keep on doing so for years to come. But didn't it also stretch back, even while seeming to happen for the first time, in a certain place on a certain day, while happening too all over the world at once? Wasn't 9/11 already a **trace** of Muslim hatred for the West, or a monster created by the CIA come back to wreak unholy vengeance on the 'friends' who'd abandoned it? As Clint Eastwood says at the end of *Unforgiven*, 'Deserve's got nothin' to do with it.' There *is* no moral periodic table to which we could refer for an explanation of what happened (or happened again) on 9/11, although a tone of what might be called the new presbyterianism adopted by many of the world's political leaders in discussions of that event would seem to suggest otherwise.

But there is also a sense in which 'the new presbyterianism' of today is simply a recent manifestation of a spectre that has haunted the history of politics. In other words, politics would be impossible *without* a moral periodic table, or at any rate without a periodic table of identifiable 'friends' and 'enemies'. This at least is the lesson that Derrida draws from a reading of the twentieth-century German political theorist Carl Schmitt, whose affinity with Nazism was a great deal less unambiguous than Heidegger's. As Derrida sees it, 'if Schmitt is to be believed, politics could never be thought without knowing *what* "enemy" means, nor a decision made without knowing *who* the enemy is. That is to say: without the *identification* by which the enemy is identified, himself, and by which one is identified, oneself' (PoF, 106). By this definition, politics demands an answer to the question, *Who's there?* Without a concept of identity understood as presence, there could be no politics. This is why Derrida's radical concept of democracy-to-come necessitates a rethinking of the political, which depends on thinking differently about what 'identity' means. In the words of John D. Caputo, this would be 'a politics which keeps on saying that the other is not this or that, not I or we, not like us or anything that is privileged by the I or we, by my place' (*Prayers*, 54). But of course even to imagine the impossibility of such a politics – a politics *of* the im-possible – one has to be in some place that is other than purely imaginary in itself. And that place, from within which it is possible to think the impossibility of democracy-to-come, is the place of democracy today. So we might say that deconstruction's avowal of the promise of a radical democracy that remains always to come is given to us from within democracy as we know it in the here and now, in the actual forms in which it has come to us from the Enlightenment. This is to acknowledge deconstruction's debt to democracy: 'no deconstruction without democracy', Derrida writes, but also 'no democracy without deconstruction' (PoF, 105). There is a hefty lesson here, in this in-dependence of democracy and deconstruction. It is that to try to think the other otherwise, to think differently about identity, is never simply 'deconstructive'; it is always also *democratic*. (See also ARTIFACTUALITY, DIFFERANCE, NEW INTERNATIONAL, MESSIANISM, ORIGIN, SUPPLEMENTARITY, VIRTUALITY.)

**differance**   The difference between differance (with an 'a') and differ-ence (with an 'e') is inaudible. Whatever might be called the meaning or identity of differance, therefore, exists only within **writing**, which is to say also that it exists only *as* writing. (So much for the undeniably powerful idea that writing comes after speech, as a 'secondary' system of 'representa-tion': see **speech–writing opposition**.) From this it can be seen that the so-called meaning or **identity** of differance 'is' its difference from difference, or at least that this is one form of that meaning or identity. Differance means difference generally, then, in the sense of difference-in-general. This is not only difficult to say; it's difficult to write. For in order to write differance I have to fight against the software I am using to write this, which has been programmed in such a way that differance registers only as a 'mistake' that has to be 'corrected'. No sooner have I written differance than it disappears, its place having been taken by difference. I then have to go back to difference (to where differance was) and change the 'e' to an 'a'. Every time I want to write differance I have to override the automatic software commands, or I have to write over what has been written into the program, a program that has been designed to 'process' words. Included in that design, clearly, is the recognition of what does *not* count as a 'word' – such as differance. Hence the software I'm using is perfectly **logocentric**.

Without suggesting that it isn't useful to have this function in a word-processing package, the point is that what the software sees only as a mistake can also be seen as the operation of (and here we go again) differance 'itself'. Or as Derrida puts it in a well-known statement, differance refers to 'the systematic play of differences, of **traces** of differences, of the *spacing* by means of which elements are related to each other' (P, 27). This is what differance means. It means, for example, not just the space *between* 'a' and 'e', but the *spacing* that makes possible the difference between them – what we might call the spacing *of* difference and *as* difference. Differance, then, is *the spacing of and as difference*. In this it functions passively and actively (as passive space and active spacing) at the same time, which is why Derrida calls it both 'a **structure** and a movement' (ibid.). The ongoing *movement* of differance disturbs the idea of difference meaning 'a fixed difference', such as the difference, say, between a word and a non-word. In so far as that idea seems to make a powerful lot of sense, we can see that the disturbance caused by differance is far from trivial. It runs, for instance, all the way through our ideas of truth, **presence**, identity and so forth. In the displacement of a single letter (the substitution of 'a' for 'e'), something like the entire history of **metaphysics** is put at risk.

The risk occurs because differance, which comes before differences, dislodges the security or self-sufficiency of concepts like truth, presence and identity. First, differance shows that difference is a passive–active effect of spacing. Out of the work of spacing, differences are produced. But differences are held not only within space; they are held also within time. So the 'a' of differance 'recalls that spacing is temporization . . . by virtue of the very principle of difference which holds that an element functions and signifies, takes on or conveys meaning, only by referring to another past or future element in an economy of traces' (P, 29). Without doubt, 'a' differs from 'e'. Without differance, though, there could be no difference between those letters, or any differences at all. This is what metaphysics cannot see; instead it sees the difference between 'a' and 'e' as a difference between positive, self-sufficient or self-present elements. Metaphysical difference is always the difference between the presence or being of *this* (letter, **text**, meaning, subject, epoch, etc.) and the presence or being of *that*. For **deconstruction**, however, it is differance that *produces* the difference between this and that (and let no one say that deconstruction is prevented from saying that *this* and *that* are different) since, without spatial and temporal separation, there could be no difference. Because everything exists in relation to its spatial and temporal separation from other things, moreover, nothing can be said to exist on its own or in its own right. Nothing exists outside of difference (there is no outside-differance). Nothing is independent of its exteriority to other things in a field of spatio-temporal differences, intervals, alterities. There is no **inside** without an **outside**. Every thing is 'inside' the field or the **play** of the spatial and temporal relations 'outside' of it. This means that what a thing 'is' must include its difference or differences from what it is not; its difference belongs to 'it', inhabiting its identity. But since differences are 'neither fallen from the sky nor inscribed once and for all in a closed system' (P, 27), we need to see that ultimately (as it were) everything owes its identity to differance.

Differance marks the opening of a system of differences in which everything acquires meaning and value according to what 'we believe we know as the most familiar thing in the world' (OG, 70–1) – that the outside is not the inside. But 'without differance as temporalization, without the nonpresence of the other inscribed within the sense of the present' (OG, 71), nothing could be said to have meaning or value in 'itself'. Everything differs, which is to say that everything defers. A thing differs because what it 'is' cannot be what anything else is, but also because what it is has to do with the fact that it differs from other things. To say that something *is* is to say that *it differs*. It is also to say at the same time that, in so far as it differs, *it defers* endlessly its 'own' constitution as an autonomous or fully complete entity, whether as sign, truth, subject or the like. Differance, then, names this work of differing and deferring that makes differences possible, which is suppressed in the metaphysical idea of difference. (See also HYMEN, PLAY, PHONOCENTRISM, SUPPLEMENTARITY, UNDECIDABILITY.)

**dissemination**    Dissemination is a *way* of **writing**, or a way with words. But this 'way' is not quite of the order of a *style* understood in literary terms, one that we might associate, for instance, with a certain avant-garde tradition of linguistic exuberance and an attitude to writing that regards it as fully immersed in the facticity of life. As Alexander Trocchi puts it in *Cain's Book* (1960), that bible of junkies and Kathy Acker-lytes everywhere: 'I always find it difficult to get back to the narrative. It is as though I might have chosen any of a thousand narratives. And, as for the one I chose, it has changed since yesterday. I have eaten, drunk, made love, turned on – hashish and heroin – since then. I think of the judge who had a bad breakfast and hanged the lout' (39–40).

For Trocchi, then, the falsity of narrative appears in the gap between aesthetic order and the sheer facticity of life. For writing to be 'honest', it cannot let itself be cut off from the 'letting be' (as **Heidegger** might say) of **beings,** from things as they are.

Again, though, dissemination is not quite a literary style, but certainly it is a way with words. This is clear from the 'book' called *Dissemination* in which Derrida never really makes an attempt at defining dissemination as such. You can show it but not quite know it, as it were. At any rate you can't quite know what dissemination 'is' (and, as we'll see in a minute, you can't quite know what *Dissemination* 'is' either) from within a way of thinking – the **metaphysics** of **presence** – which tells you that everything has to have a determined meaning. You could of course look up dissemination in a (**proper**) dictionary, where you'd be told that it means to scatter and to sow, but what dissemination 'means' in (and as) *Dissemination* is not reducible to that.

Here is the opening sentence of *Dissemination*: 'This (therefore) will not have been a book.' As Barbara Johnson notes, the sentence is 'written in the future perfect tense, marks itself as presentation ("this"), anticipation ("will"), negation ("not"), recapitulation ("have been"), and conclusion ("therefore")' ('Preface', p. xxxii). No doubt something (a sense, perhaps, or the sense of a sense) is 'sown' here, but all the same the meaning of the sentence is 'scattered' in several directions at once. This – a plurivocal drive or energy – discloses not so much a theme or an intending consciousness, or a particular stylistic approach, but a force within writing itself. And given the insuperably unruly and enabling nature of that force, it would be impossible to try to define or thematize dissemination. Hence to look for the meaning of dissemination 'in' *Dissemination* would be to search in vain.

But of course Derrida's fascination (taking his cue from Joyce, perhaps) with the waywardness, the ineluctability and the aleatoriness of words, does not mean he thinks that words have no meanings. He thinks they have too many meanings, or at least so many that no one could ever be their master. This was the view, too, in a sense, of the modernist avant garde, of writers such as Joyce, Mallarmé, Kafka and Genet, whom Derrida admires greatly. And perhaps what he admires about them is that in their work the force of dissemination is let loose; there is no attempt to resist or suppress it. The point rather is to allow language to disseminate 'itself', to let meanings proliferate, to keep open as many possibilities as it is possible to keep open at once. Such a writing calls into question what 'writing' means, what 'literature' means, and while that questioning has a romantic history (see Lacoue-Labarthe and Nancy, *Literary Absolute*, and Lucy, *Postmodern*), the more vital source for Derrida is the writing of the modernist avant garde of the first half of the twentieth century or thereabouts.

To use a shorthand, this avant-garde sense (which is also a romantic one) of writing as the *question* of writing is expressed in the work of dissemination, and of *Dissemination*. It is in this sense that Derrida's dissemination is a *way* of writing, a way with words. While this 'way' cannot avoid being thought of as 'literary', nonetheless it is irreducible to a *style* understood in terms of literature as such; indeed the work of dissemination disrupts the comforting idea that every concept – the concept of literature, for example – must have an ideal form and purity that is all its own. And so after the writings of Joyce, Mallarmé and others, which might be said to show that the disseminatory force of language is an 'ordinary' feature, a precondition, and not a special 'literary' form of language, there is a sense in which the concept of literature is rendered obsolete, out of date, quaintly historical. As Derrida asks, 'why should "literature" still designate that which already breaks away from literature – away from what has always been conceived and signified under that name – or that which, not merely escaping literature, implacably destroys it?' (D, 3).

Similarly, a certain *way* of writing (one that is not reducible to a form of literature) can unsettle the form and concept of 'the book' understood according to a notion of overall unity – unity of style, unity of theme, unity of purpose. In its refusal of that unity, *Dissemination* (and dissemination) refuses the book's presence, or the idea that every book has its own self-contained **identity**. There are ways of writing, then, that no book could contain: 'the book form alone can no longer settle – here for example – the case of those writing processes which, in *practically* questioning that form, must also dismantle it' (ibid.). Given that *Dissemination* is written in many styles (rhetorically and typographically), such excess undoes a notion of the unity of the book.

But note that dissemination is a force within language already, before an author may be said to choose to write any particular book in a particular style. Hence the opening sentence of *Dissemination* is true of every book in general: 'This (therefore) will not have been a book.' From the very beginning, in other words – indeed *before* any beginning – dissemination is at play, such that every book 'will not have been a book' from the very first inkling of an idea. Whatever it will have been when it is 'finished', it will not have been a book (organized around a concept of unity), though of course the work of dissemination always remains ongoing and can never be finished with. As the unruly and enabling force of language (the force of writing and **textuality** in general), dissemination happens always in the middle of things, without **origin** or telos, before every beginning and past every end.

It might be said that Derrida learns the lesson of dissemination from literature, even though part of the lesson is that 'literature' is not an especially meaningful term these days. All the same it is from literature – the least pedagogical of discourses, as it were – that Derrida could be said to learn a lesson. The point here is that we cannot afford to think along the lines of a division between literary texts giving pleasure and philosophical texts containing ideas – this indeed is one of the lessons of *Dissemination*, and dissemination. As what always happens in the middle, the work of dissemination undoes the order of things, disrupting the security of borders and regulations and unsettling the solace of ideal forms. Dissemination refuses the ontology of presence. But at the same time the force of dissemination makes it seem possible that presence is in everything, that every thing has a purity or self-constitution belonging to 'it' alone.

In literature, of course, a certain order of semantic indeterminacy is a desirable effect of a certain way of writing. But this is not the case in philosophy, where writing serves a 'higher' aim of bringing us to some truth that exists 'outside' any particular *way* of writing. For philosophy, writing is a medium or vehicle for getting to the truth; hence the disseminatory force within writing is something that philosophers seek to suppress. What might be said to be the point of Derrida's *Dissemination*, however, is to show that a way of writing (a 'style', as it were) can never operate exclusively at the level of the signifier – ways of writing are not reducible to styles. This is true of philosophical writing as well, which may choose to ignore dissemination but nevertheless cannot avoid it, no matter how stubbornly it holds to an idea of writing as representation and hence to the possibility of being able to write in such a way that what is written seems transparent.

The lesson of *Dissemination*, then, is that dissemination is not just what happens in literature (or as literature). Dissemination is not (simply) a way of writing, and of course it is nothing but a way of writing. While this may indeed be the 'lesson' of *Dissemination*, nonetheless it is important to remember that dissemination is not a theme; it's a practice. Dissemination is what happens. And it happens just as inexorably in philosophical discourse (unsettling and enabling the signification of truth) as it does in literary discourse. One way of showing this is to read philosophy and literature 'against' themselves, which Derrida does in *Dissemination* by reading Plato for his use of words and the poetry of Mallarmé and the avant-garde writing of Phillipe Sollers for their ideas. This is done, of course, only to undo the notion of a determined opposition between literature and philosophy, or between words and ideas. What this calls for is a 'double' reading, one that acknowledges a certain limit to the interplay of literature and philosophy, figure and concept, representation and non-representation, only to transgress that limit. Hence the linguistic exuberance of *Dissemination* – the 'stylistic' apparatus of puns and word-games, the lexical and typographical variations and so on – constitutes a way of writing that is also a way of reading. To see this way (or this double way) as belonging both to a certain tradition of the avant garde and to philosophy in its canonical sense (textually inventive and conceptually rigorous, as it were) would be to see it as a ***pharmakon*** effect, or in terms of non-oppositional difference. The work of dissemination (and *Dissemination*), then, does not lead to relativism; instead it opens the possibility of encounters with others, including but not restricted to philosophy's encounter with literature (and vice versa). (See also DIFFERANCE, HYMEN, ITERABILITY, PLAY, SPECTRALITY, SUPPLEMENTARITY, TRACE, UNDECIDABILITY.)

**event** The feature story in the 'new millenium' issue of the British music monthly *Uncut* is entitled 'Apocalypse Wow! 100 Moments that Shook Music, Movies . . . and the World', written by Nick Hasted. The list makes for fascinating reading, because what it seeks to record as instances – or events – of world-historical significance are, in most cases, too seemingly ephemeral to count as history in the standard sense. Take the entry for Bob Dylan's world concert tour in 1966, the year that Dylan 'went electric'. Every night in every hall the hecklers started up when Dylan finished his acoustic set and began performing with The Hawks (who later became famous in their own right as The Band). As Hasted sees it, this never-ending return of the same is encapsulated in one defining moment that 'comes down to posterity as a single night: the Manchester Free Trade Hall, May 17, 1966' ('Apocalypse', 46). On that night, with the concert nearly at an end, 'a heckler spears Dylan to the spot: "JUDAS!" A staggered pause, then, Dylan: "I don't *believe you*!", and, gleeful, "You're a *liar*!" "Like A Rolling Stone" pounds in, Technical Knock Out, and Dylan hardly has to ask his tormentors: "How does it *feel*?"' (ibid.).

But what exactly is being recorded here? What kind of an *event* is this? For Hasted its significance amounts to a lesson in courage: 'Little since', he writes, 'has sounded so brave' (ibid.). But since when? Since that 'moment' in Manchester, lasting either only a couple of hours or scarcely a minute, on 17 May 1966? Or since the event of the whole tour itself that year? And to what extent does the event-ness of the event depend on Dylan's diffuse and abiding influence on popular music – not only in terms of the singer-songwriter tradition, but also as a kind of **spectral** effect in the music and attitude of bands such as The Sex Pistols and Sonic Youth, Nirvana and Primal Scream – as though every musical 'revolution' after the Manchester concert, every 'new' sound or movement, from punk to hip hop, were somehow a repetition of that night when Dylan said, 'I don't *believe you!*'?

There is no need to answer these questions, at any rate not here. But certainly it seems fair to say that the event-ness Nick Hasted and *Uncut* accord to that night in Manchester in 1966, when perhaps Dylan was not the only person in the city to have said, 'I don't *believe you!*', is very much bound up with Dylan's world-historical significance as a kind of quasi-political or counter-cultural icon. To some extent, then, the Dylan entry in *Uncut* conforms to a standard concept of event-ness: the date assigns it a certain time; the venue, a certain place. There were witnesses. This thing actually happened.

Defined by the fact of its spatio-temporal specificity, the event seems full of **presence**. There, in that place on that night, someone in the audience said this, Dylan said that, and then the band played 'Like a Rolling Stone'. Clearly, though, the event is irreducible to a spatio-temporal fact. The significance of any event – the event-ness of an event – simply is *not* present in a place or a date, whether it be Manchester, 17 May 1966, or Manhattan, 11 September 2001.

And event-ness – the significance of an event – is always **artifactual**; it is always something that is *made*, which is not to say it is always 'made up' in the sense of being opposed to whatever is regarded as actual or to what counts as a fact. Defined from within the **metaphysics** of presence, however, events always appear as things in themselves, and not as things that have been made or produced. According to the metaphysical concept of event, every event happens outside of the **text**, outside of representation. In practice, though, certain normalizing procedures – of language, politics, the media, etc. – produce certain occurrences as events, and overlook the event-ness of others. Outside a certain spectral community of those for whom music is vital to their sense of **being** in the world, and not simply a commodity, it would seem to be drawing a long bow to claim any world-historical significance for what happened at the Dylan concert in the Manchester Free Trade Hall on 17 May 1966. To claim what happened there and then as an event, let alone to claim that it is happening still, would be precisely to be seen as *claiming* something, to be *making* a case, to be *producing* what happened on that night in Manchester (which is happening still) as something deserving of world-historical attention and worthy of entry into the historical record. In a word, Manchester, 17 May 1966, is not Manhattan, 11 September 2001.

True, but what *is* the event of Manhattan, 11 September 2001? What is 9/11? Now of course there are many claims (and counter-claims) concerning the event-ness of 9/11; we don't need to list them here. The point is that 9/11 is not self-evidently any more world-historical than Dylan's concert in Manchester in 1966, or indeed any other event; but certainly it has been made to seem so. Certainly, too, it seems impossible (because metaphysics makes it seem that way) to think that an event involving the death of thousands of people is not more significant than a musician shouting 'I don't *believe you!*' at a heckler during a concert. Or – and this would be to make a difference – perhaps the event-ness of the Manchester concert should be couched in terms of the artist shouting 'I don't *believe you!*' at the world. It would make another difference to claim this as the artist saying '**yes!**'. This is not a 'postmodern' argument; this is not about the relativity of all things; it is not a specious attempt to justify not having to take **responsibility** for the suffering of others, as if the event-ness of 9/11 were the same as that of Dylan's 'bravery' in 1966. (It should be remembered, however, that his 'bravery' is not reducible simply to a verbal retort, a public statement of conviction, the 'romantic' artist expressing himself in defiance of any need for audience approval – for two members of The Hawks, Levon Helm and Al Kooper, had quit the tour before the night of the Manchester concert, in fear of their lives.) It is, on the contrary, precisely out of a respect for the responsibility to others, out of the in-dwelling of each of us with every other one of us who lives, who is no longer living and who is yet to live, that it is necessary to question a concept of event defined in terms of presence.

As Derrida tells it, this involves having to rethink the concept of event outside the opposition of actual and virtual, real and imagined, presence and absence. Such an event, the rethinking of event, cannot happen – it cannot be thought –

> as long as one relies on the simple (ideal, mechanical, or dialectical) opposition of the real presence of the real present or the living present to its ghostly simulacrum, the opposition of the effective or actual (*wirklich*) to the non-effective, inactual, which is also to say, as long as one relies on a general temporality or an historical temporality made up of the *successive* linking of presences identical to themselves and contemporary with themselves. (SoM, 70)

In this context the Dylan entry in *Uncut* both does and does not conform to a standard concept of the event. As an isolated moment in time,
it belongs to an idea of historical temporality comprising 'successive'
instances – or instants – of presence; and in this it is standard. But in so
far as its event-ness has to be claimed, to be argued for, to be *made* –
because it does not seem to belong self-evidently 'outside' the text, having
therefore to be brought or made over 'into' text – the Dylan entry is not
quite straightforwardly a standard case of the general concept of an event.

Such are the events that interest deconstruction – events that go
unnoticed from within the metaphysics of presence; that don't make
it into history books, aren't reported on TV, don't feature in political
campaigns or have no official place in bureaucratic or institutional discourses, but which nonetheless go to make up the facts of life. This, the
spectrality, the 'here and now-ness' of life – the facticity, the artifactuality,
the **virtuality** of living – is what prevents any event from ever coming to
presence. But to think of being and time – to conceive of life – in terms
only of the opposition of life and death, the actual and the virtual and so
on, is to condemn many events in the world today to the order of the
unpresentable – not as **Kant**'s sublime, acting as 'an outrage on the imagination' (see *Judgement*), but as what cannot be seen and cannot therefore
be said, because it cannot be assigned a time or a place within a schema of
'the world' defined by an idea of 'historical temporality made up of the
*successive* linking of presences identical to themselves and contemporary
with themselves'.

Again, the example of the Dylan entry in *Uncut* serves to show that
things 'happen' – this, for John D. Caputo, is the minimal condition of an
event (*Ethics*, 93–8) – but in so far as things are accorded any significance,
they never happen outside the text. An event, then, is whatever happens.
Hence the exchange between Dylan and his audience in Manchester in
1966 is an event, but this is not to say that to see it as such it must be
necessary to think (as it were) deconstructively, or to think through
**differance**. The *Uncut* entry is instructive, because according to a certain
ideal of history it has the status of being an unorthodox example of an
event, but all the same it still belongs to 'an historical temporality made
up of the *successive* linking of presences identical to themselves and contemporary with themselves'. More radically, Derrida's rethinking of the
**structure** of an event involves a 'deconstructive thinking of the **trace**, of
**iterability**, of prosthetic synthesis, of **supplementarity**, and so forth' in
order to see that 'the possibility of the reference to the other, and thus of

radical alterity and heterogeneity, of differance' is always already inscribed 'in the presence of the present that it dis-joins' (SoM, 75). If, let's say, 'radical alterity and heterogeneity' are the condition that make the concept of presence possible, and if presence is necessary to the metaphysical concept of the event, then we can say that without presence understood in opposition to 'radical alterity and heterogeneity' (trace, iterability, supplementarity, etc.) there could be no event as such. Without the idea of presence as absolutely self-sufficient, an absolute ground, a fixed, unshakeable centre or essence, there could be no concept of *the event as presence*, 'identical' to and 'contemporary' with itself.

Set loose from metaphysical constraints, events are free to become what happens. Events defined in terms of presence happen 'outside' the text. But, for **deconstruction**, to 'see' an event is also to *make* it. And this involves having to make decisions – a decision to see, to make, the event in the first place, and to make decisions about, to make arguments for, its significance. Events defined in terms of presence, which happen outside the text, outside 'the ordeal of **undecidability**' (SoM, 75), leave no room for decision-making and hence no room for responsibility. Wrapped in the security of an historical date attached to an actual place, metaphysical events ask ideally to be described rather than interpreted. But deconstructive events are effects – texts – of active interpretation, effects of interpretative activities, of thinking beyond the opposition of the actual and the virtual. This is why, among other examples of unreported facts, Derrida lists the 'massive exclusion of homeless citizens from any participation in the democratic life of States' and the 'aggravation of the foreign debt and other connected mechanisms [that] are starving or driving to despair a large portion of humanity' as *events* that are happening in the world today (SoM, 81–2).

Now, of course, it isn't necessary to have to undergo a programme of training in deconstruction in order to see, and to say, that there are injustices in the world at present, or that poverty and deprivation are effects of inequitable politico-economic forces. To want to see and to say such things it is necessary only to have been born into the time and place of the Enlightenment. And so for instance, writing in 1950, one of the twentieth century's great champions of the Enlightenment, the British historian Isaiah Berlin, was able to see and to say, without ever having read any Derrida, that what is called for by what we have inherited from the likes of Kant and Condillac and Voltaire is this – 'less Messianic ardour, more enlightened scepticism, more toleration of idiosyncracies, more frequent *ad hoc* measures to achieve aims in a foreseeable future, more room for the attainment of their personal ends by individuals and by minorities whose tastes and beliefs find (whether rightly or wrongly must not matter) little response among the majority' (*Essays*, 39–40). As Berlin saw it, and had the conviction to say, the middle of the twentieth century was in the grip of a terrible world-historical event – the dominance of conformity. A time that should have been marked by progressive optimism, on the back of the promise of the New Deal and the defeat of Fascism, was marked instead, as Berlin saw it (or *made* it seem), by an ancient, 'spectral' force – 'the tendency to circumscribe and confine and limit, to determine the range of what may be asked and what may not, to what may be believed and what may not' (*Essays*, 37). For Berlin, then, the post-war world was 'stiff with rigid rules and codes . . . , it treats heterodoxy as the supreme danger' (ibid.).

These words are not inconsistent with many things Derrida has written, in the name of deconstruction, in defence of difference. The lesson to be drawn from this is not that we should think of Berlin as a proto-Derridean, but that Derrida – no less than Berlin – believes in such Enlightenment ideals as **justice**, **democracy**, equality, non-violence and what might be called a sort of intellectual equanimity. He believes, in a word, in letting things 'be' what they 'are'. And it *'must not matter'* whether they are judged moralistically to be right or wrong. But still they must be judged. How then to judge things that happen – events – outside an authoritarian grid or system, whether moral, political, sociological, psychological, philosophical, etc.? How is one to be true to the Enlightenment imperative to judge – to be involved, to be critical, to take a stand, to stand up and speak out against implacable authority – in the absence of a transcendental ground from which to do so?

To see judgement as necessary is to see it from within the time and place of the Enlightenment. But to see it as a question – a question that must pass through 'the ordeal of undecidability' – is to see it from somewhere and someplace else, which might be called the continuation of the Enlightenment by other means: the post-Enlightenment, as it were. The benighted view of deconstruction as apolitical, socially uncommitted, relativistic and so on, fails to take account of deconstruction's manifest avowal of a certain spirit of the Enlightenment – the will to question – whose various animations and conjurations are conjoined diversely in resistance to the possibility of a future defined by the dominance of conformity, 'the tendency to circumscribe and confine and limit, to determine the range of what may be asked and what may not, to what may be believed and what may not'. For Derrida, the best means of defence against that tendency is to attack its resources – its conceptual reservoir of ideas, values, logic. That is why he insists on having to rethink the fundamental concepts of metaphysics, such as the concept of event, because it is precisely through those fundamental concepts that it has come to pass, in our time, that all around us in the world today there is the 'massive exclusion of homeless citizens from any participation in the democratic life of States'. (See also GIFT, HEIDEGGER, ITERABILITY, MESSIANISM, NEW INTERNATIONAL, POSTAL METAPHOR, TELETECHNOLOGY, WRITING.)

**Freud, Sigmund** (Austrian physician, 1856–1939)   I suppose it's just the luck of the draw. You wake up one morning with something as irritating as Elton John's 'I Guess that's Why They Call It the Blues' (1984) playing in your head, and the next morning you've got something as sublime as The Ronettes' '(The Best Part of) Breakin' Up' (1963) inside there.

But if events like this are not entirely random, could there be a scientific explanation for them? In other words, what could be going on when we're asleep, so that we often wake up with a song, a thought or an image in our mind that we may or may not want to have, but which we didn't bring about consciously? More generally, what is the nature of the psyche such that we are not always in control of what we might be thinking or feeling?

This of course was Freud's question, and he claimed that the answer to it lies in an understanding of the unconscious. 'The unconscious', he wrote, 'is the true psychical reality' (*Dreams*, 613). Now this can be taken in a couple of ways: it can mean that the unconscious is a kind of underlying **presence**, hidden from consciousness but able to be 'unveiled' by psycho-analytic treatment, or it can mean, more radically, that the unconscious is effectively untranslatable. In this latter sense the unconscious is a form of what Derrida calls **differance**, a non-originary **origin**. The unconscious is not simply a dark reservoir of 'repressions'; it is also activated by repression. As Derrida points out, the radical 'otherness' of the unconscious cannot be understood as a series of 'modified presents', as if the unconscious were a stockpile of formerly conscious experiences (MoP, 21). A psychic 'dis-order', say, does not necessarily have an objective or actual 'cause' in the form of an event that was once present. Hence for Derrida the unconscious functions as a **text**; its **structure** and its operations are textual.

But if the textuality of the unconscious is the **proper** object of psycho-analysis, this raises questions for psychoanalysis as a discipline. How can psychoanalysis claim any disciplinary authority if its objects and methods are closer to those of literary criticism than to science? For there can be no doubt that Freud, as the 'father' of psychoanalysis, wanted his life's work to be regarded as the basis of an authoritative explanation of the workings of the human psyche. To this extent he wanted psychoanalysis to be seen as a discipline modelled on the sciences. Yet at the same time there could be no hope of explaining scientifically an 'object' which Freud characterized in terms of what he called 'overdetermination', or what Derrida calls **supplementarity**, **undecidability** or the **trace**-like **play** of differential mean-ings. Meaning, for Freud, is always 'overdetermined'; it is never the product of a single determining cause. As Joseph H. Smith and William Kerrigan argue, this is where 'Derrida's deepest, though ambivalent, indebtedness to Freud' is revealed ('Introduction', p. ix). For if there is never any point at which meanings could leave differance (the play of differing–deferring) behind and come into presence, then no meaning is ever fixed and final. This play is both the condition of meaning and the condition of the impossibility of absolute meaning. In the absence of overdetermination or supplementarity, then, 'no definite meaning could be and because of it no meaning can be absolutely definite – and no discipline as well' (ibid.).

So Derrida sees the Freudian enterprise both as an attempt to engage speculatively and imaginatively with the nature of overdetermination and as an attempt to establish psychoanalysis as a discipline. By taking overdeter-mination as its object, psychoanalysis is necessarily involved with 'taking chances': it 'analyses' only by risking an interpretation. But by privileging the work of interpretative activity as its distinguishing 'disciplinary' feature, psychoanalysis risks not being seen as a discipline at all. At any rate it risks being seen as a discipline only in the weakest sense – like literary criticism, for example.

Psychoanalysis can never afford to settle for heading in just one of these directions. To go the way of endless speculation would mean having to forsake disciplinary legitimation; to go the way of theoretical mastery would mean having to forget that psychic overdetermination is indomitable. In this sense psychoanalysis has to go on playing the game of 'fort-da' – a game which Freud observed his grandson playing on one of the many occasions when the child's mother (Freud's daughter, Sophie) was absent from her son. The game consisted of the grandson (Ernst) repeatedly throwing away from his cot and then reeling back in a bobbin attached to a piece of string. As Ernst threw it out he uttered the sound 'fort' (meaning 'gone', according to Freud) and then, as he reeled it in, he uttered 'da' ('back', 'there'). Freud took this to mean that Ernst was reassuring himself that his mother would always come back to him even though she was gone for now and no doubt would go away again (see Freud, *Beyond*). The story is told in the context of Freud's theory of the psychic balance that must pertain between a desire for pleasure and the denial of gratification; in other words the story is caught up in a system of massive speculation, which puts at stake the credibility of psychoanalysis as a discipline. As Derrida reads it, Freud himself is playing the fort-da game here by offering an adventurous interpretation ('fort') which he brings back reassuringly ('da') into the framework of evidential material for a general theory of the human psyche. Psychoanalysis itself, moreover, always seems to have to come back to the 'father', even though a science 'should have been able to do without the family name Freud' (COO, 142).

In a word, psychoanalysis can't let go of thinking that the relations between waking up with 'I Guess that's Why They Call It the Blues' and waking up with '(The Best Part of) Breakin' Up' must be coded; they can't be put down to chance. 'The attempt to submit chance to thought', Derrida writes, 'implies in the first place an interest in the *experience* (I emphasize this word) of that which happens unexpectedly' (MC, 5). The **event** of waking up with a certain song in your head is an instance of something that 'happens unexpectedly'. Now, as Derrida puts it, 'unexpectability conditions the very structure of an event', since 'an event that can be anticipated and therefore apprehended and comprehended' would not 'actually be an event in the full sense of the word' (ibid.). But, like superstition, psychoanalysis is driven by a 'hermeneutic compulsion' (MC, 22) to apprehend events and to comprehend their meanings. 'Freud says it explicitly. He does not believe in chance any more than the superstitious do' (ibid.). As Freud remarks in *The Psychopathology of Everyday Life*: 'I believe in external (real) chance, it is true, but not in internal (psychical) accidental events. With the superstitious person it is the other way round' (cited in MC, 23). So what Freud believes in is 'scientific objectivity', Derrida argues, which he opposes to the 'credulity' he associates with superstition (MC, 23–4).

Such a belief presumes to know the limits separating the scientific from the superstitious, which is the basis on which Freud is able to present the psychoanalytic project as 'a positive science'. Chance is thus eliminated from the psyche. 'There is no chance in the unconscious', as Derrida puts it. 'The apparent randomness must be placed in the service of an unavoidable necessity that in fact is never contradicted' (MC, 24). But in its avoidance or refusal of the effectivity of chance, psychoanalysis is forced to return the explanation of events to a 'scientific' discourse as determined by **metaphysics**. This is the field or discourse '*from which it nonetheless obtains the concepts themselves for this project* and operation – notably, the oppositional limits between the psychic and the physical, the **inside** and the **outside**, not to mention all those that depend on them' (MC, 27). This is not to say that Derrida opposes deconstruction to psychoanalysis, for in fact he has no single position on what psychoanalysis could be said to mean politically or intellectually. But generally speaking he is critical of its scientific aspirations, which always in the end and from the start limit the radical force of its interpretative possibilities. Freud is a recurring figure in Derrida's work; see *Writing and Difference, Margins of Philosophy* and *The Post-Card* for some key discussions. (See also ARTIFACTUALITY, BEING, DISSEMINATION, INTENTIONALITY, SPEECH–WRITING OPPOSITION.)

**ghost**  See **spectrality**.

**gift**  In a sense, there is no such thing as a gift. But then for me, since I don't believe in them, there is no such thing as a ghost either, though I've never been able to bring myself to see the film *The Blair Witch Project* (1999) for fear of being petrified. So to say that we cannot say of some things 'there is' does not mean that nothing remains to be said about them, as if a thing's non-phenomenality disqualifies it from having any kind of reality, force or signifying power at all.

Yet surely there are such things as gifts – I gave out several last Christmas, and received several in return. And there's the rub. Each time you give someone a gift, you and the other person are inscribed in an economy of exchange. You feel good about yourself for giving, and he or she is grateful to receive. At that very moment the gift begins to disappear.

In the act or movement of giving and receiving, there is no gift. Or rather since the gift is something that must, from the very beginning, come back (in the form of an expression of gratitude or a return gift), it is already gone from the start. It never comes 'to be', remaining always 'to come'. The gift consists of this disappearance, this non-presence, this **aporetic** mode of being. In what we can call the 'real time' of any giving, the gift 'annuls itself' (GT, 30) or is rendered impossible once it is given in exchange for something else – an equivalence in the form of the giver's feeling of pleasure, for instance, or the receiver's 'thank you'. Within this economy or circle of exchange, the gift 'itself' disappears. But the desire to give something without getting anything back – the gift in all its impossible purity – is precisely what inaugurates the economy of exchange; the gift in this impossible sense is the 'exteriority that sets the circle going' (ibid.). Hence we can say that there 'is' something like the *moment* of the gift, but it is not a moment that exists in real time. This does not mean that the 'groundless ground' of this moment, of what the gift 'is', should be taken for a transcendental essence, though, as if the gift existed only in some kind of ideal exteriority beyond all reach of reason or what Derrida calls 'the *principle of reason*', even if that principle 'finds there its limit as well as its resource' (GT, 30–1).

So by acknowledging the impossibility of the gift, we are not required to leave the economic circle behind. The gift does not pose (or impose) a choice between itself and economy, any more than **justice** forces a choice between itself and the law. Like justice, the gift is that impossible something that exceeds and makes possible the **structure** of an opposition (giving and receiving, say). And in this strange ontology, in its impossible temporality, the gift resembles death. For death is always absolutely singular. No one can die another's death; no one can take away the death awaiting someone else – 'dying can never be taken, borrowed, transferred, delivered, promised, or transmitted' (GoD, 44). Throughout my life the moment of my death remains to come, as mine alone, for me only. No one can take that moment from me, and I cannot give that moment to anyone else (not even to myself). To die for another is to give something that is impossible to give, which is why death displaces the opposition of giving and taking – making it possible to give, without giving, the gift of death. Such a gift is inexpressible as anything other than itself, unable to be translated into an idiom that makes sense to **metaphysics**; and certainly it cannot be thought to occur inside a notion of history as **presence** or 'real time'.

Nor can it be thought within or be made present to 'lived experience', 'real life' or the conscious intentions of a living subject. Before anything can be imputed with a sense of self-sufficient unity or an **identity** of its own, it has to pass through the 'ordeal' of **undecidability** (FoL, 24); for anything to appear *as such* (as itself, in its own right), it has to have begun, in a seemingly impossible sense, from the possibility of never appearing as such. And if this impossible possibility is inscribed in the constitution of everything that 'is', then it cannot be seen as incidental to the structure of a thing's identity (its presence, reality, **being**, etc.). The impossible possibility (or the possibility of the impossible) belongs to that structure, doubling and dividing the identity of everything that is.

A desire for the impossible can of course take may forms. Depending on your age and gender, for example, it could take the form of wanting to look like Tony Curtis in *The Sweet Smell of Success* (1958) – making you almost willing to kill for that haircut, that jacket, that way of moving in the world. But such a desire could never be realized, because to succeed in imitating the way Tony Curtis looks and moves in the film would also be to produce a difference (**iterability** always leads to alteration). You could never quite look like Tony Curtis *in* the movie *The Sweet Smell of Success*; even the best imitation of his role in that film would have to be played out somewhere else, in another context. And this would be true even if Tony Curtis were to imitate himself. So a desire to look like Tony Curtis in *The Sweet Smell of Success* is impossible, which is why someone might harbour such a desire.

It is this 'experience of the impossible' (FoL, 15) that may be said to drive **deconstruction** to press against the limits of the opposition of presence and absence, actual and virtual, reality and representation and so on. In this regard the figure of the gift, which is outside the opposition of what might be called an economy and an ethics of giving, functions as another example of the limits of metaphysics. A gift that was given simply out of obligation (to fulfil a duty to your father, say, on Father's Day) could never count as a gift in any meaningful sense; rather it would be an object that was presented to the other according to a set of predetermined or programmed rules. You cannot give a gift when you hand over something to the other in order to satisfy the conditions of an economic transaction or because duty dictates that something is owed to the other on a certain day or for a certain reason. A gift is always more than what is due. But the impossibility of the gift lies in the fact that it cannot exist outside a circle of exchange, beyond all reach of protocol or without any desire at all to receive pleasure as a result of giving pleasure to the other. Hence there is no 'pure' gift but only ever different economies – economic variations – of gift-giving. To open the economic circle, to move as far away as possible from the constraints of protocol and obligation, would be to approach the 'purity' of the gift. (See also ARTIFACTUALITY, DEMOCRACY, HYMEN, INTENTIONALITY, *PHARMAKON*, POSTAL METAPHOR, RESPONSIBILITY, TEXT, TRACE, WRITING, VIRTUALITY.)

**Heidegger, Martin** (German philosopher, 1889–1976)   While Heidegger's influence on Derrida's thinking cannot be overstated, all the same there are two general 'ways' or directions in Heidegger that Derrida doesn't follow. These can be put as the way back to the 'primordiality' of **Being** and the way forward to the 'gathering' of beings under Being. Each of these ways belongs, for Heidegger, to the time of the early Greeks (before **Plato** and Aristotle), when 'thinking' had not yet been compartmentalized into 'disciplines' like philosophy, physics or literature. So if today you want to know about ethics, for example, you wouldn't go looking for 'specialist' statements about ethics under the general rubric of the discipline of philosophy: you'd go back to the early Greeks, before 'ethics' had a name. 'The tragedies of Sophocles', Heidegger writes, '– provided such a comparison is at all permissible – preserve the *ethos* in their sagas more primordially than Aristotle's lectures on "ethics"' ('Letter', 233). As Derrida might see it, the problem here would have to do with notions of preservation and primordiality, both of which are forms of **presence**.

The other Heideggerian direction (towards 'gathering') is perhaps an even bigger bone of contention with Derrida. While Derrida acknowledges that '**deconstruction** owes a lot to Heidegger' (VR, 14), he makes it clear that his ongoing debate with him 'has to do with the privilege Heidegger grants to what he calls *Versammlung*, gathering, which is always more powerful than dissociation' (ibid.). Every gathering overlooks the singularities of others, collecting different differences as the same. This is why Derrida is always on the side of what might be called a de-ontologizing force of dissociation, **dissemination** and **differance**. Every instance of a gathering, 'whether or not it is on the basis of Being as presence and the property of the **proper**', as Derrida puts it, fails to acknowledge what must

> be rendered to the singularity of the other, to his or her absolute *precedence* or to his or her absolute *previousness*, to the heterogeneity of a *pre-*, which, to be sure, means what comes before me, before any present, thus before any past present, but also what, for that very reason, comes from the future or as future: as the very coming of the **event.** (SoM, 27–8)

In its 'heterogeneity', in other words, such a '*pre-*' is not to be thought of as 'primordial' and so it cannot form the basis of any future 'gathering' that would always be a return to some half-remembered 'authenticity' of the past, when (for example) Sophocles knew more about ethics than Aristotle. Derrida's discussion of Heidegger is recurrent and extensive, but see *Of Spirit* for a sustained account of the relations between Heidegger's philosophy and 'politics'. (See also DEMOCRACY, METAPHYSICS, RESPONS-IBILITY, SPEECH–WRITING OPPOSITION.)

**hymen**   Men do not have hymens; it might even be that this is what they 'lack'. Perhaps, then, Derrida's interest in the figure of the hymen indic-ates a certain thinking of the feminine on his part, such that femininity (which need not be understood as female 'subjectivity') is constituted or played out *in medias res*, happening only in the in-between. The hymen, he writes,

> merges with what it seems to be derived from: the hymen as protective screen, the jewel box of virginity, the vaginal partition, the fine, invisible veil which, in front of the hystera, stands *between* the **inside** and the **outside** of a woman, and consequently between desire and fulfillment. It is neither desire nor pleasure but in between the two. Neither future nor present, but between the two. (D, 212–13)

So men's 'lack' (or the lack in 'man' as the very subject of subjectivity) may reside precisely in the absence of this spatio-temporal movement, or this 'hymeneal' **play**, within a concept of the subject understood in terms of unity, plenitude and **presence**. Such a lack or absence could be an effect only of suppressing the work of **differance**.

But while men do not have hymens, neither does the hymen belong to women (or to woman). Tracing its Greek and Latin etymologies, Derrida contends that 'hymen' carries a general sense of 'membrane' or 'tissue' (referring to the bodies not only of people, but also birds, fish and insects) and is related to 'sewing', 'weaving' and 'spinning' (D, 213). Once again, in other words, the hymen 'merges with what it seems to be derived from' – it *is* this 'weave' of etymological **traces** and differences. Its etymology constitutes what Derrida calls a 'hymenology' or 'hymenography' (ibid.), which for him is true of etymologies in general. Every word is hymeneal, that is to say; its etymology is always a hymenology, a tissue of meanings without an absolutely central or **proper** meaning against which other meanings could be marked off as 'exterior'. In the case of the word 'hymen' itself (and of course the work of 'hymeneality', as it were, presses at the very limits of the notion of an 'itself'), it is situated *in between* sexual and non-sexual meanings. It is not tied to woman's 'vaginal partition' since its threads extend to 'textile, spider web, net, the **text** of a work' (ibid.). The hymen does not belong on one side or the other of the sexual/non-sexual partition: it 'is' the partition. It 'is' the web, the net, the text.

'The hymen is thus a sort of textile', Derrida writes, referring here to the work of the French poet Stephane Mallarmé (1842–98), albeit the point holds generally (ibid.). We might say that its ontology (if it has one) is fabric-ated, made up of ontologically flimsy fibres, threads and traces. For Derrida it stands for everything that is barely ontological, everything within the spatio-temporal interval between the presence of *this* and the presence of *that*, such as the time and space between virginity and non-virginity. 'At the edge of **being**', he writes, 'the medium of the hymen never becomes a mere mediation or work of the negative; it outwits and undoes all ontologies, all philosophemes, all manner of dialectics' (D, 215). Again the reference is to Mallarmé, but the general point is that the hymen is situated neither on the inside (of a body, a work or whatever) nor on the outside. So where and what 'is' it? What exactly is the ontology of something that is marginal, or the ontology of the margin 'itself'? What is its time and place? What is the 'being-there' of a margin?

The point is not to try to find answers to these questions (certainly there are none that **metaphysics** could provide) but rather to see that the questions have force. Whatever the strange ontology (or quasi-ontology) of the margin, it cannot be construed in terms of presence. Yet if not for margins, how could we separate an inside from an outside? We might not be able to say for sure what kind of a thing a margin is, but surely it is some kind of a thing. So to concede the force of the questions that are being asked here is to begin to 'de-ontologize' ontology, or at least to weaken its authority. It's to acknowledge that the work of the margin is essential to the imputed ontology of an inside (or an outside), and what is an ontology that is also an *effect* – an effect of something prior to 'itself'?

All 'marginal' work is hymeneal, in the sense of operating both on and between the relations of any inside to an outside. Take the example of female corporeality, which is not reducible to the 'presence' of the hymen any more than it's reducible to the 'lack' of a penis. But at the same time a woman's body is constituted in its difference from a man's body by virtue of a necessity which in itself is marginal: the hymen is what must be present in the form of the lack of presence. This might be to conceive of female subjectivity, based on the vestigial or vestibular nature of female corporeality, in terms of an openness to the other, an openness that both divides and belongs to the self. Grounded on the 'groundless' or quasi-transcendental ground of 'difference within', rather than 'difference between', subjectivity begins to unravel or to de-ontologize itself. The subject who is other than 'the complete man' is not quite a subject at all. But if it turns out that difference within is the groundless ground of difference between, then we might say that the subject who is lacking, in fact, is 'man'. It is not woman who lacks a penis, but man who lacks a hymen: his subjectivity (which is to say subjectivity itself) lacks or suppresses any acknowledgement of what might be called the enabling force of self-difference. Woman's 'lack' is positive and pro-ductive, in other words, such that the very idea of man's 'completion' is an effect – and not a correction – of an originary self-difference or difference within. And this originary difference (or differance) is of course what Derrida associates with **writing** as the groundless ground of speech or 'being' understood as presence (see **speech–writing opposition**). For Derrida, then, the figure of the hymen is a kind of 'non-synonymous' synonym (or analogue) of writing, along with a series of other terms including differance, trace, **dissemination, undecidability**, etc. Or as the French writer and philosopher Hélène Cixous puts it, 'writing is the passageway, the entrance, the exit, the dwelling place of the other in me that I am and am not, that I don't know how to be, but that I feel like passing, that makes me live – that tears me apart, disturbs me, changes me, who?' (Cixous, *Reader*, 42). In this way to write as a woman may be to write 'hymeneally' or 'hymenographically', as it were, in the sense of writing from a subject 'position' which is less a position than a movement.

The hymen as the veil or tissue in general (and not exclusively a membrane belonging only to women) occupies a sort of 'non-space' between an inside and an outside, yet it also helps to determine the differences between insides and outside *as* determined differences. Without such a movement there could be no position: you could never take up a position from 'inside' somewhere (subjectivity, say) or be accused of standing on the 'outside' of a thing (the truth, for example). So the figure of the hymen describes this movement or work of joining and separating, connecting and dividing – it describes what happens in the non-locatable, non-determined 'place' of the in-between. This is the place of writing, too, since writing is what always happens between intentions and effects, inscriptions and significations, authors and readers, presence and representation and so on. Like the hymen, writing is ontologically veiled; its 'being-there' is of the order of what is barely there at all. Presence, being, **identity** – these are understood to lie behind the veil, as if they were always already in place from the start. But Derrida's point is that the hymen does not come 'after' subjectivity and it doesn't 'mediate' between the body and the self. Writing does not come after speech or mediate between the presence of a subject's intention and the absence of the subject. Neither writing nor the hymen is an after-effect, and the work they perform is not of the order of mediation but of **supplementarity** The supplement, the hymen, writing – these all work to open the possibility of a concept of the subject understood in terms of presence, dividing what they produce, erasing what they enable at the same time. (See also APORIA, FREUD, ITERABILITY, GIFT, *PHARMAKON*, SPECTRALITY.)

**identity**  For anything to have an identity, differences have to be gathered or lumped together as the same. Let's say that my identity were given in terms of being an Australian English-speaking man; in that case it would seem obvious that my identity must differ from that of a Canadian French-speaking woman. So to claim any shared identity between us – as 'Westerners' – would mean having to overlook any differences between us. But surely each of the identity-markers I have just used – nationality, language and gender – is replete with differences rather than being full of **presence**. Regardless of the language they might speak and irrespective of gender, in other words, not all Australian adults would want to write (or will want to read) *A Derrida Dictionary*, just as not all Canadian adults would want to record or buy a CD as salacious as the Canadian dance artist Peaches' *The Teaches of Peaches* (with song titles like 'Lovertits' and 'Fuck the Pain Away'). The fact I happen to enjoy listening to Peaches doesn't make me un-Australian; the fact that some Canadians may (I hope) enjoy reading *A Derrida Dictionary* won't make them un-Canadian.

This argument goes all the way down, as it were. Take the identity-marker of a language 'itself'. As an Australian I don't speak English as such; I speak Australian English (I don't get sick, I get 'crook'). But this doesn't mean that Australian English is somehow implacably homogeneous: like every language, it's happy to appropriate or accommodate so-called foreign words and phrases. And this is not a consequence simply of 'defiance' on the part of 'immature' speakers, since for every Australian teenager who uses 'motherfucker' nowadays there's an Australian corporate executive who always writes 'disc' instead of 'disk' and has a 'trash can' in the bottom corner of his or her computer screen. The same could be said for every other version of 'English', as for every other language. When it comes to languages, immigration policies don't work – you can't keep the others out.

The point is that Australian teenagers who say 'motherfucker' are no less 'Australian' than their parents, who may or may not say 'motherfucker', but who, like their children, delete their computer files by dragging them to the 'trash'. Nothing is atomically essential when it comes to nations or languages. Yes, there is a sense in which 'Australianness' does mark a certain identity, but mainly with respect to differences: to be Australian is not to be British or Japanese, etc. By the same token one may be 'Australian' in many different ways, which is to say that 'Australianness' differs not only from other national identities but also *within* 'itself'. Similarly, every language is different within 'itself' and from other languages, just as there are no 'core' features belonging to a gender. John Wayne, Mick Jagger and Boy George are all men, for instance, but what they represent collectively about 'masculinity' is that it's full of differences within. To claim that masculinity has a single or homogeneous identity (in opposition to femininity, say) would necessitate all the differences between the likes of John Wayne, Mick Jagger and Boy George having to be gathered or lumped together as the same.

Derrida insists that 'self-difference' structures every identity. 'There is no culture or cultural identity [for example] without this difference *with itself*' (OH, 9–10). Every invocation of an identity (the identity of **democracy**, of a nation state, of a language, etc.) has to occlude the fact that no identity is ever identical to 'itself'. Again, there are many ways to be Australian – just as there are many ways of being masculine or feminine and so on. These ways – these differences – constitute identity in terms not of a 'gathering' but of a 'divergence' (OH, 10). What Derrida says of culture, then, is true of identities in general: '*what is **proper** to a culture is not to be identical to itself*' (OH, 9). (See also DIFFERANCE, HYMEN, INSIDE–OUTSIDE, KHORA, PHARMAKON, SAUSSURE, SPECTRALITY.)

**inside–outside**    I know that when I'm holding a glass of water in my hand the water is *inside* the glass and my hand is *outside* the glass. Countless other examples could be chosen to make the same point – that there is a distinction between 'inside' and 'outside' and everyone knows what it is. This is true for practical purposes, in the sense that it 'works', but it is not true always and everywhere. By the same token the appearance of a certain determined or transcendental difference between inside and outside is essential to thought understood as **metaphysics**. But it can be shown that, as a ground, the nature of this difference takes the form of complex and shifting relations, thereby displacing its groundedness.

While the necessity of a seemingly transcendental difference between inside and outside is a 'permanent requirement' of thought in general, Derrida argues that it reveals itself especially in all understandings of art. 'This permanent requirement – to distinguish between the internal or **proper** sense and the circumstance of the object being talked about – organizes all philosophical discourses on art, the meaning of art and meaning as such, from **Plato** to Hegel, Husserl and **Heidegger**. This requirement presupposes a discourse on the limit between the inside and outside of the art object, here a *discourse on the frame*' (TP, 45). Derrida is writing on this occasion about **Kant**'s theory of the aesthetic, but note that by 'permanent requirement' he refers to an activity: what is required is the work of having to distinguish between the inside and the outside of any art object. This activity, this work, is what frames perform, which may seem obvious in the case of paintings but is no less effective in regard to other aesthetic objects. So we might say that the work of the frame (framing work) meets the permanent requirement of making it seem that the difference between inside and outside is transcendental – not *made*, but natural.

Derrida focuses on Kant's distinction between the Greek terms *ergon*, or 'work', and *parergon*, or 'outside the work' (what in French is called *hors d'œuvre*) in order to show the problem of situating the frame in terms of that distinction. As Derrida notes, *hors d'œuvre* can be translated also as '"accessory, foreign or secondary object," "supplement," "aside," "remainder."' It is what the principal subject *must not become*' (TP, 54). The essential originality and integrity of the *ergon* depends therefore on the essential secondariness of the *parergon*, or depends on its **supplementarity**. But where is the place of the frame in this relation, since the frame belongs neither to the *ergon* nor on the outside? Kant himself saw this as something of a problem and thought to resolve it by making the frame into a special *parergon*, 'a hybrid of outside and inside, but a hybrid which is not a mixture or a half-measure, a hybrid which is called to the inside of the inside in order to constitute it as an inside' (TP, 63). The inside of the work (its essential originality and integrity) is given to it by the work of the frame, though of course Kant did not see this. Nonetheless, for Derrida it is framing work that separates *ergon* and *parergon*; the *ergon* is produced by the work of the frame. To be constituted as a work in itself (full of an essential originality and integrity) the *ergon* must be set off against a back-ground, and this is what the frame works to achieve. More generally, though, this is what the *parergon* achieves, so that we can think of framing work in terms of what Derrida calls the work of 'parergonality' in general. Parergonality (framing work) is outside-work: the *ergon* is an effect of the *parergon*.

This outside-work (the outside at work on the inside, as it were) will pose a problem for any theory of aesthetic judgement, whose proper object must always be the work (*ergon*) itself. 'Hence one must know – this is a fundamental presupposition, presupposing what is fundamental – how to determine the intrinsic – what is framed – and know what one is excluding as frame *and* outside-the-frame' (TP, 63). The frame then is at the limit or on the border separating the intrinsic from the extrinsic, and at the same time the intrinsic (the *ergon*) is precisely *what is framed*. It follows from this that there can be no theory of the art object as such, but only a theory of the whole field (what Derrida sometimes calls 'the general **text**') in which the art object is produced or constituted. And that field opens out from somewhere in the in-between, between the *ergon* and the *parergon*. Both for Kant and aesthetics generally the *parergon* is always separated from 'the integral inside, from the body proper of the *ergon*' and from the outside in the widest sense: the outside of a painting for example is not just 'the wall on which the painting is hung' but includes the painting's separation, 'step by step, from the whole field of historical, economic, political inscription in which the drive to signature is produced' (TP, 61). The artist's compulsion to sign for the originality of his or her work (a compulsion 'outside' the work), in other words, is inseparable from the general text of historical, economic and political interests that are served by the concept of originality tied to the concept of the individual. All of this belongs to the general text of the history of **being** understood as **presence**.

This is to say that the separation of the aesthetic from the non-aesthetic is related to the separation of the self from others. I could not think of myself as having desires, a personality, a set of values and so on belonging to and constituting my **identity** as an individual, without thinking that the outside is *not* the inside and vice versa. So when Derrida argues that no theory or practice of art can afford to overlook the work of parergonality, the force of that argument is not restricted to its effects on discourses about art. No discourse on art, Derrida insists, could hope to have anything to say about the field in which artworks and the concept of art are produced, 'if it does not bear up and weigh on the frame, which is the decisive **structure** of what is at stake' (TP, 61). But the necessity to account for framing work is a lesson not only for aesthetic discourse, since it is precisely the 'invisible' work of the frame that produces a general distinction between 'theory' and 'empiricism'. The frame is 'at the invisible limit to (between) the interiority of meaning', on the one hand, which is the object of theory, and on the other '(to) all the empiricisms of the extrinsic which, incapable of either seeing or reading, miss the question completely' (ibid.). Hence the 'permanent requirement' to separate the inside from the outside 'organizes all philosophical discourses on art, the meaning of art *and meaning as such*'. The theory of semiotics, for instance, presupposes that *parole* (any signifying act) is inside *langue* (the system of differential relations that makes signifying acts possible); or – same difference – *langue* could be said to be inside every act of *parole* (see **Saussure**). But it would make a great deal of difference to the *langue–parole* distinction if the very nature of inside–outside relations were understood as parergonal or **undecidable**.

Similarly, Husserl's phenomenological distinction (see his *Ideas*) between *epoche* (the 'bracketing' of existent theories of the world) and 'pure immanence' (phenomena as they are) could not be sustained in the absence of a strict distinction between what is intrinsic and what is extrinsic to the 'transcendental subjectivity' of everyday experience. But this is not to say that **deconstruction** is against phenomenology, any more than it's against semiotics (or structuralism), though it may be to acknowledge that deconstruction is both post-phenomenological and post-structuralist in the double movement of its debt to and deviation from a decentring of the subject (phenomenology) and a decentring of the sign (structuralism). Nor could it be said that by taking issue with the *ergon–parergon* distinction in the Third Critique, Derrida commits deconstruction to opposing Kant.

There simply is no question about Derrida's admiration for the ideas of Kant, Husserl and Saussure (in a long list of others, not all of them philosophers or theorists). The deconstruction of the self-constitution of the *ergon*, then, is inseparable from its involvement in a larger or greater enterprise: the deconstruction of identity. And that enterprise is not about cancelling or erasing identity (concerning the *ergon*, the sign or the subject); it's about the *ungroundedness* of identity – the necessity, which might be called an ethico-political necessity, of not allowing identity to be fixed or grounded in, or tied to, a notion of presence. To leave identity at that would be to leave things as they are, which would mean to keep on demanding (for example) that 'Palestinian' identity should have to keep on accounting for and justifying itself to an identity-standard defined by Israel, the United States or the West. For there to be 'world-historical' change there has to be change within metaphysics. That's the point of intervening in the general structure (and Kant's version) of the inside–outside opposition. (See also DIFFERANCE, EVENT, GIFT, HYMEN, JUSTICE, *KHORA*, ORIGIN, *PHARMAKON*, SPECTRALITY, TRACE, WRITING, VIRTUALITY.)

**intentionality**    Derrida has never said that authors (or sign-users generally) don't have intentions, or that intentions don't have effects. In his notorious 'debate' with American speech-act philosopher John R. Searle (see my *Debating* for the details), however, it is precisely this – the 'non-intentionality' of textual production and the 'limitless' interpretability of **texts** – that Searle accuses Derrida of promoting, speciously, as the implacable conditions of every act of communication. Hence we can never know (on Searle's interpretation of Derrida's intended argument) what anything means because no one ever intends anything by a communicative act, and so there are no limits to what something might be interpreted as meaning.

Derrida has never said that authors don't have intentions, or that intentions don't have effects. What he has said on the question of intentionality is this: rather than seeing plain, ordinary, everyday language in opposition to special kinds of language use (for citational, literary or other purposes); rather than seeing the **iterability** of language in opposition to the purity of language, 'one ought to construct a differential typology of forms of iteration' (LI, 18). No speech act would be possible, in other words, indeed it would be impossible to use any sign or **mark**, unless it were able to be repeated: this 'iterable' quality is the precondition of every speech act, etc. Derrida derives this point from the American philosopher of 'ordinary' language J. L. Austin, the actual (intended) meaning of whose work Searle believes himself to be upholding in his criticism of what he sees as Derrida's perverse misreading of Austin. On Searle's view, while Austin concedes the preconditionality of iteration, nonetheless he regards it as a trivial matter in comparison to the serious philosophical work of accounting for the different principles and features of different types of speech acts. Briefly, Austin's argument (supported by Searle) is that we can rule out consideration of the 'special' effects of 'performative utterances' (statements that are not intrinsically true or false but only ever 'felicitious' or sufficient within a certain context) when it comes to knowing what a speaker means by what a speaker says. On this model, ordinary language is originary and all performatives (fictive speech acts, for example) are derivative, parasitic, secondary or **supplementary**. Derrida's position, though, is that because iterability (or iteration) is a communicative precondition, which holds in every case, then in fact the notion that somehow there is a form of communication ('ordinary' language) that 'escapes' this precondition, invests that form with a 'special' status. Because all language use, including ordinary language, is subject to effects of performativity, then to see ordinary language as immune to those effects is to make a case for it to be seen as a special kind of language use. Instead of holding on, then, to an untenable opposition between iterable ('performative') language use and 'non'-iterable ('ordinary') language use, we should think of language use (or sign usage generally, or textuality) in terms of 'a differential typology of forms of iteration'.

Note that this does not cancel intentionality. 'In such a typology', Derrida writes, and later repeats, 'the category of intention will not disappear; it will have its place, but from that place it will no longer be able to govern the entire scene and system of utterance [*l'enonciation*]' (LI, 18 and, with 'the category of intention will not disappear' in italic, 105). There can be no doubt about this: to regard all utterances as performative, or to see supplementarity as originary; to dismantle the opposition between iterable and effectively non-iterable utterances, or to see the opposition as a secondary effect of iterability – this does not, Derrida says, lead to the cancellation of intentionality.

Surely only a complete idiot would think we don't have intentions when we say, or try to say, what we mean. Derrida's point is simply that having an intention is one thing; being understood to mean what you say (even if you're the one who's doing the understanding) is another. The first thing cannot guarantee the second. Intentionality has a place in communicative acts, but it cannot 'govern the entire scene and system' of signification or what Derrida calls **writing**.

'The first consequence of this' is that because of the necessity of iterability, the intentionality of any utterance 'will never be through and through present to itself and to its content' (LI, 18). Hence it turns out that, far from trying to do away with intentionality, the point of Derrida's intervention into Austin's notion of ordinary language is to undo **presence**. His target is not what might be called a general concept of intentionality as such, but the **metaphysical** concept of *intentionality as presence*. Without a concept of intentionality as presence there could be no concept of 'ordinary' language – together, then, these concepts 'shelter a lure, the teleological lure of consciousness' (ibid.). The idea that ordinary speakers using ordinary language always say what they mean and mean what they say gives the strong impression that consciousness determines meaning. So at least two effects can be ascertained from the argument that performativity 'determines' meaning (in indeterminate and **undecidable** ways): first, that consciousness is not a determining ground of meaning and, secondly, that there *is* no determining ground of meaning. These effects are not quite separable, but let's concentrate on the first for now. Without a notion of determining consciousness, any theory of 'the subject' is put at risk. What is a 'subject' (as an individual, a singular **identity**, the Cartesian *cogito* and so on) without a determining consciousness? This is not quite to open a notion of subjectivity as determined by the indeterminate operations of the unconscious, albeit that is not entirely beside the point here. Indeed, as Derrida remarks, we might compare the necessity of iteration to a certain 'structural unconsciousness, if you like', which would prevent any context from leading to a 'saturation' of meaning or from becoming 'exhaustively determinable' (LI, 17). All the same the more pressing point is that if consciousness does not determine meaning, this weakens all versions of the concept of subjectivity.

Note that this does not cancel subjectvity. Nor does it relocate it in some other, quasi-determining and quasi-determinable, place – the unconscious, for example. Derrida's argument against what might be called a notion of grounded and grounding intentionality and consciousness has as its purpose an unsettling of the metaphysical concept of presence as foundational centre or impervious essence, and it's no accident that the metaphysical concept of the subject is a casualty of that argument. But there could be no sense in which we would be able to do without a concept of subjectivity altogether, any more than we could think that simply by critiquing presence we would be able to do away with it once and for all. If the **deconstruction** of intentionality involves the deconstruction of subjectivity, this is only to open (in a word) the possibility of a concept of **spectrality**, and to do so in the name of **justice** and **democracy**. And if the figure of the spectre forces us to think of being outside the opposition of life and death, it does not do so by cancelling all possible senses of what it means 'to be' alive. Nor does the concept of a general performativity cancel all possible effects of intentionality. 'By no means', Derrida writes, 'do I draw the conclusion that there is no relative specificity of effects of consciousness, or of effects of speech (as opposed to writing in the traditional sense)'. He has never claimed that presence, ordinary language or speech acts have no effects at all. His claim instead is that, whatever those effects might be, they cannot be understood to 'exclude what is generally opposed to them, term by term; on the contrary, they presuppose it, in an asymmetrical way, as the general space of their possibility' (LI, 19). (See also FREUD, HEIDEGGER, LOGOCENTRISM, PHONOCENTRISM, POSTAL METAPHOR, SPEECH–WRITING OPPOSITION.)

**iterability**   First thing every morning I make myself a cup of coffee; in fact I make several cups. Each coffee is singular, unique, unlike the others (the second cup is not the first and so on), but each one is also an instance of the same, the general, the others that it resembles and to which it belongs. This is not a feature peculiar to coffee; it's a condition of the singularity of a thing – any thing – that the thing in itself belongs to a general form of such things which that particular thing represents. Everything is always therefore a **trace**, a **text**, an example of **writing**.

This means that for a thing to be what 'it' is, it must be able to be repeated. Every sunset is a sunset in itself *and* an example of sunsets in general. Tonight's sunset will be followed by another sunset tomorrow, and while each of these will have its singularity, they will also both be the same. In a sense, tonight's sunset will be repeated tomorrow night, but in the very fact of being tomorrow night's sunset it will not be exactly the same as it was tonight. Every repetition, then, produces a difference. This **structure** of sameness-and-difference conditions every singularity, which can always be repeated. The important point to notice here is that repetition is never pure; it always leads to alteration. To repeat something is to alter it, to make a difference.

In so far as everything can always be repeated, then the condition of repeatability (repetition in general, as it were) belongs to every thing in 'itself', contaminating or compromising its purity. This is why Derrida uses the term *iterability* to refer to this condition, because his point is not simply that things can be repeated in an empirical or factual sense, but rather that in order to be what they are they have to be conditioned by this possibility – a possibility that makes them always less or other than what they 'are'. Iterability refers to this structure of repetition-as-difference, which both enables and limits the idealization of every single thing's singularity, purity, **presence**. This is true of iterability itself. As a concept, iterability has to have an ideal singularity (a meaning unto itself); in this way every concept is always an ideal concept. But what iterability means is that nothing can exist entirely unto itself, in a state of perpetual 'once only-ness', never to be repeated (even if it never is repeated as an empirical fact). And it is iterability that makes it possible to think that something could exist only in its pure and absolute singularity. Therefore, as Derrida puts it, iterability is both 'an ideal concept' and 'also the concept of the possibility of ideality' (LI, 119).

For something to happen for the first time, it is already possible for it to happen again (whether or not it actually ever does so). Everything originates in this 'already-ness' that both pre-exists and preconditions every **origin**. This is the origin as the trace, the non-origin that was never present but is never non-existent. Hence the **identity** of every thing (as concept, subject or **event**), which depends on everything having an origin, depends on the structure of iterability that both structures and unstructures the ideality of 'its' identity. No doubt this is a difficult way of thinking about things. But to ignore this difficulty, for the sake of 'clarity' or 'simplicity', would be to risk a dangerous purification that might be just as political as it could be philosophical (or vice versa). 'Those who wish to simplify at all costs', Derrida writes, pose as much risk as 'those who wish to purify at all costs' (LI, 119). The **logocentric** ideal of a concept's self-presence, for example, necessitates a reduction of the concept to its ideal and fails to see the concept's ideality as a textual effect or projection, since the ideal 'itself' is forever 'inaccessible' (LI, 117). The lesson here (not only for philosophy) is that concepts are never outside of writing or the text; their ideality depends on their iterability, and this disturbs any notion of a concept having a fixed 'centre' of meaning that remains impervious to 'marginal', 'secondary' or 'metaphorical' meanings. The structure of iterability, then, makes it impossible to distinguish absolutely between 'pure' philosophy and 'pure' literature – or between logic and rhetoric, referent and sign, concept and figure and so forth.

Each term in the foregoing series of pairs owes its identity to a structure that comes before the term itself, such that in order to have an identity, first of all each term has to be iterable (alterable). The term 'philosophy' could not be said to 'contain' the concept of philosophy if the marks that make up the term cannot be recognized as letters belonging to the English alphabet and arranged in such a way as to constitute that term. But they could not be recognized as such unless it were possible for them to be repeated; this is the minimal condition of possibility of every word or sign, for a word or a sign that could not be repeated (altered) could not be recognized or function as a word or a sign. This possibility also conditions every concept. So it isn't that, once formed, a concept leaves this possibility behind, establishing an identity for itself by superseding or overcoming the structure of iterability. The possibility that both divides and produces every identity always also inheres in every identity. In its non-present (but not non-existent) inherence, the structure of iterability prevents every concept from reaching a final or an absolute form. Concepts never arrive; they always keep on be-coming.

Quickly rounding up in order quickly to eliminate the usual suspects here, the concept of iterability doesn't commit Derrida or **deconstruction** to nihilism, relativism, obscurantism, apoliticism, egoism, mysticism, narcissism or the vandalism of all values and beliefs. But the concept does serve to show that ideas concerning value and belief and so on are not grounded on pre-given structures of meaning or difference. Since Derrida admits to ideality (even to the ideality of the concept of iterability), how could he ever be against values and beliefs, as if to say that anything goes? Rather than seeing iterability in opposition to ideality and identity, then, we should see that, as the precondition of ideality and identity, iterability is opposed to the *certitude* of ideals, the *dogma* of beliefs, the *self-assurance* of identities and the *constancy* of values. (See also PHONOCENTRISM, PLAY, POSTAL METAPHOR, SPECTRALITY, SPEECH–WRITING OPPOSITION, YES.)

**justice**  'Are you drinking to get maudlin', David McComb sings in The Triffids song 'The Seabirds' (1986), 'or drinking to get numb?' It's a rhetorical question, of course, and you aren't meant to answer it. But the thing about so-called rhetorical questions is that they constitute a special class to the extent only of being understood to differ from a standard form – questions that do require an answer. Now while it is entirely reasonable to expect that questions should be answered, it would be wrong to think that every answer always puts an end to the matter in question. It is one thing to expect to receive an answer to a question, but quite another to accept without question the answer that is given.

This doesn't mean that answers have no validity at all; it means they are not predetermined. At any rate there are no predetermined answers when it comes to having to respond to questions that require you to make a decision, especially an ethical one. For example: questions concerning justice, if not the question of justice itself.

What would it mean if there was no absolutely definitive answer to the question, *What is justice?* What would be the consequences for a legal system which took that question seriously? Could it still function?

No doubt we should put this to the legal profession. But less than half an hour ago, as it happens, I came across an item in today's issue of my local paper that puts the question for us. The story concerns a mooted proposal by the State Government of Western Australia to abolish the 'double jeopardy' law, which holds that once you've been acquitted of an offence you cannot be tried for that offence again. (Anyone who's seen the Billy Wilder film *Witness for the Prosecution*, released in 1957, will be familiar with the principle.) What does the legal profession think of this proposal? Despite the headline ('Lawyers Back Double Jeopardy'), it would seem the jury is still out. The President of the State Law Society is reported to oppose any change, because the law's removal 'would mean there would be no guarantee the verdict of a court was final', while the State Director of Public Prosecutions is in favour of changing the law. The Director is quoted to have said he thinks 'the time has come for a more rational view to be taken on whether or not we should retry people who have been acquitted' (Gregory, 'Lawyers').

The disparity here between the headline's declaration of absolute unanimity and the story's inclusion of two opposing views is not uncommon. It's an old news trick, which cultural studies brought to our attention a long time ago (see Hartley, *News*). But in this case, without having to invoke a conspiracy, we could speculate that the headline makes sense once public prosecutors are excluded from the category 'lawyers', as presumably they must be for the staff of *The West Australian*. So let's say that the legal profession's view is that the abolition of the principle of double jeopardy would result in there being 'no guarantee the verdict of a court was final'. The day's editorial endorses this view by making the strongest case for retaining the double-jeopardy principle (though it also finds a case for removing it) on the grounds that it provides 'an affirmation of confidence in the justice dispensed by the courts' (Editor, 'Merit'). What would 'acquittal' mean, in other words, if someone who had been acquitted of a charge still stood at risk of having to answer to that charge again at another trial? Where would this end?

That's not a rhetorical question. The case for double jeopardy is all about finality and ends, about finding answers, about being able to say there comes a time when 'the law has run its course' (ibid.). The 'confidence in the justice dispensed by the courts' depends on the finality of their verdicts. If courtroom decisions were seen as anything less than final, if they were seen as speculative or provisional responses to legal questions, they may as well be wild guesses. Courts are there for shedding light on the truth, not for taking stabs in the dark.

But the problem (as Derrida sees it) is that while it may be one thing to attribute a kind of pragmatic finality to courtroom decisions, it is quite another to suppose that, in their finality, such decisions must be just. This points to a distinction between the absolute undeconstructibility of justice, on the one hand, and the actual deconstructibility of the law on the other. A verdict seen as arbitrary or whimsical would never be seen as just; and so there is no question (on Derrida's account) that justice is not outside the law in a transcendental sense. But while justice is never absolutely outside the law, neither could we say there must be justice once 'the law has run its course'. We cannot think that justice remains to come until the court settles on a verdict, at which time there is justice. Out of respect for its radical undeconstructibility we cannot afford to think of justice as something that happens in the present – as something belonging to **presence**. We could never say that, at this very moment, there is justice. Derrida writes:

> There is apparently no moment in which a decision can be called presently and fully just: either it has not yet been made according to a rule, and nothing allows us to call it just, or it has already followed a rule – whether received, confirmed, conserved or reinvented – which in its turn is not absolutely guaranteed by anything; and, moreover, if it were guaranteed, the decision would be reduced to calculation and we wouldn't call it just. (FoL, 24)

Reduced to an effect of calculation, justice becomes a foregone conclusion and ceases to be a question.

No one has to take any **responsibility** for a 'foregone conclusion', which appears always as an answer waiting to be found, waiting to come into the present, as though nothing had to be decided at all. In this way justice seems inevitable: it comes when the law has run its course. But if the question of justice demands not only our responsiveness but always also our responsibility, then justice cannot be defined as the necessary outcome of a legal process. There is always work to be done when it comes to the question of justice, and this work – the work of invention and interpretation – cannot be handed over to 'the law' or any calculating system or programme. As Derrida puts it, 'for a decision to be just and responsible, it must, in its proper moment if there is one, be both regulated and without regulation: it must conserve the law and also destroy it or suspend it enough to have to reinvent it in each case, rejustify it, at least reinvent it in the reaffirmation and the new and free confirmation of its principle' (FoL, 23). Justice always keeps us waiting, in other words; it always remains to come. The radical and absolute irreducibility of this 'to come' opens an idea of the future that cannot be understood in terms of a repeated present: *to come* defers *there is*. 'Justice remains, is yet, to come, *à venir*, it has an, it is *à venir*, the very dimension of **events** irreducibly to come' (FoL, 27).

There is no sense in which Derrida is calling on us to let the future happen willy-nilly, without any regard for injustices in the here and now. On the contrary, the point of insisting on the undeconstructibility of justice (on the radically unforeseeable future it makes possible and keeps open) is to emphasize the manifest deconstructibility of the law, or the deconstrucibility of events which are happening in the world today that have been sanctioned by legal processes or justified by political systems. Such events include not only (as I write) the impending invasion of Iraq (where everything awaits the moment of United Nations approval, vested with the authority of international law) but also economic deprivations, trade inequites, civil-rights infringements and the like, all of which can be reinterpreted, reinvented and redirected because none of them is grounded in undeconstructible presence. (See also DECONSTRUCTION, DEMOCRACY, INSIDE–OUTSIDE, *KHORA*, POSTAL METAPHOR, SPECTRALITY, UNDECIDABILITY.)

**Kant, Immanuel** (German philosopher, 1724–1804)   More than perhaps any other philosopher of his day, Kant has come to epitomize the Enlightenment. But it is important to remember that in his famous essay 'What is Enlightenment?' (1784) he stressed that while he might have been living in what could be called 'the Age of Enlightenment', he was not living in enlightened times as such. In other words, superstition still abounded in the realm of the everyday, though it was true that reason and good sense had begun to make some inroads into cultural life. Although Kant may have been optimistic about the future, he was still in a sense waiting for the Enlightenment to happen, still waiting for its philosophical insights to become 'common knowledge'.

As Kant tells it, then, we should not think of the Enlightenment as belonging only to a philosophical tradition or to the historical past. From this we might say that the Enlightenment is still 'happening' (or still waiting to happen) today, which does not mean that a line of perfect intellectual continuity should be drawn from Kant to 'us'. All the same, as far as Kant's influence on Derrida is concerned, it can at least be said that **deconstruction** has an affinity with 'the age of criticism', misconceptions to the contrary notwithstanding. If deconstruction is not quite a form of critique or criticism in 'itself', certainly it is not the opposite of these. If Derrida has sometimes taken Kant's ideas to task (see especially *Truth in Painting*), it has not been in order to pave the way for 'relativism' or to sound the death of 'reason'.

The main problem Derrida has with Kant concerns the latter's faith in the purity of 'transcendental' questions, which ask after the conditions, the preconditions or the presuppositions of knowledge. Kant argued that epistemological pursuits should be conducted on the basis of a priori or transcendental rules of inquiry, which belong to us already in the immanent form of 'intuition'. The human mind contains the conditions of perception ('intuition') for making sense of the external world, and so things in the external world can never be known to us 'in themselves' but only through our regulating perceptions. Our thinking, as it were, gets in the way of our being able to know the world directly. There is clearly an affinity here between Kant's argument against the possibility of accessing the 'noumenal' (the realm of things-in-themselves) and Derrida's persistent disruptions of the idea of **presence**. For all that, we need to see that Derrida departs from Kant when it comes to the question of what grounds moral law.

In the famous ending to the *Critique of Practical Reason* (1788), Kant refers to 'the starry heavens above me and the moral law within me' as two such powerfully awe-inspiring things that he claims to be able to 'see them before me'. His very sense of **being** is inseparable from knowing that there *is* a universe and there *is* morality. These are no doubt awesomely grand things to be thinking about, but they tend not to be the sorts of things that occupy a lot of Derrida's time, given that he doesn't seem to believe that faraway planets shine much light on the question of **justice**, for example, or act as guiding stars with respect to our **responsibility** towards the absolute singularity of others. But for Kant the regulated movements of the stars above correspond to the immanent regulations of human consciousness, which enable subjects to give to themselves laws which are at the same time universal. Such giving or willing involves not only rational thought but also the imagination. One has to imagine (in a 'disinterested' fashion) what a universal law would look like, while at the same time willing that law into existence. The way to do this is to make a decision as if there were a universal ground for making it and as if the outcome were directly accessible to the mind. Any such decision would be free and responsible, according to Kant.

For Derrida, the problem here has to do with the all too neat and tidy separation of immanence and transcendence. 'Each case is other,' he writes, 'each decision is different and requires an absolutely unique interpretation, which no existing, coded rule can or ought to guarantee absolutely' (FoL, 23). Any decision made on the basis of a presuppositional or preconditional law would not be just (because it would not be 'absolutely unique'); it would not even be a decision, but simply the enactment of a prior regulation. But neither could a decision be called just if it were made with complete disregard for laws, on the basis of pure intuition or opinion. 'It follows from this paradox', Derrida continues, 'that there is never a moment that we can say *in the present* that a decision *is* just (that is, free and responsible), or that someone *is* a just man – even less, "*I am* just"' (FoL, 23). The immanent regulations of human decision-making, then, do not pass over into transcendental ideals. Asking 'transcendental' questions won't guide you towards justice. Instead, the **inside–outside** relations of the limits separating law and justice (or other Kantian 'antinomies', such as immanence and transcendence or the phenomenal and the noumenal) constitute for Derrida 'an unsurpassable **aporia**', as Drucilla Cornell puts it. 'Justice, in other words, operates, but it operates as aporia' (*Philosophy*, 133). (See also DEMOCRACY, DIFFERANCE, SUPPLEMENTARITY, UNDECIDABILITY.)

**khora**    This is almost but not quite ancient Greek for 'anything goes', or so it would seem following Derrida's reading of the conceptual and semantic slipperiness of this term (whose supposed meaning is 'place' or 'location') in **Plato**'s *Timaeus*. Where is the place of the *khora* (or *chora*) itself in the philosophical scheme of things? What is its definition? Any attempt to fix or locate answers to these questions would have to ignore that what is precisely and at the same time paradoxically essential to the *khora* is its 'textual drift' (ON, 123). Where is the place of what is always on the move? As Derrida sees it, then, *khora* is that third thing (between the intelligible and the sensible) that makes it possible to think anything like the difference between pure **being** and pure nothingness (or between my autonomous selfhood and your autonomous otherness); it is what makes it possible to think the difference between 'I' and 'you'. To be brief, *khora* is the pre-philosophical, pre-originary non-locatable non-space that existed without existing before the cosmos. Something like that. Derrida refers to it as 'a necessity which is neither generative nor engendered' (ON, 126). Its singularity – and this is the point – is its very resistance to being identified; it is what philosophy cannot name. But since philosophy can't quite face up to being powerless to name something (what would it mean for philosophy to know that there are things it cannot know, but which could be known intuitively, say, or imaginatively?), the 'khoral' section of the *Timaeus* has always been treated as a literary trifle and not as serious philosophy. Among Derrida's points is that Plato was being most serious of all, he was doing the hardest philosophy, when he was thinking the *khora*: in his not knowing how to name or identify what is **proper** to the *khora*, Plato had to confront the structural necessity of this 'not knowing' in the 'being' of every '**identity**'. In the end Plato, and afterwards philosophy, shunned the confrontation, but for a moment there, albeit only for a split second, one might say that **deconstruction** was right at the centre of philosophy, almost but not quite right from the start. (See also DIFFERANCE, DISSEMINATION, LOGOCENTRISM, METAPHYSICS, *PHARMAKON*, SPECTRALITY, SPEECH–WRITING OPPOSITION, SUPPLEMENT-ARITY, UNDECIDABILITY.)

**logocentrism** Some things seem to go together naturally, like pop corn at the movies. Other things – a tow bar on a Mustang? – don't. Yet the difference between contiguous and differential relations isn't natural in itself, although neither is it completely haphazard or indiscriminate. Different cultural codes and conventions bring some things together and keep others apart, and these codes and conventions have their institutional, political, regional and other histories. So when it comes to what can be called historical truth, it may be easy to concede that the way things are at present is not the way they absolutely had to be. Whatever state the world is in now, things could always have been different; and whatever picture we might have of where things are going, the future remains unpredictable.

In the formation of 'historical' truth, then, it can be conceded that a certain kind of **undecidability** belongs to it. But surely there is another order of truth, which exists outside of history and is absolute in itself. Who doesn't believe this to be true of truth? Without having to say that truth is entirely a matter of opinion, what if it turned out to be true that the belief in absolute truth also has a history of its own, belonging to what Derrida calls 'the epoch of the logos' (OG, 12) which began with **Plato** and within which we still find ourselves today?

Derrida's argument on this point concerns the founding **metaphysical** authority that Platonic truth gives to the 'absolute proximity' of voice and thought – 'of voice and **being**, of voice and the meaning of being, of voice and the ideality of meaning' (OG, 11). The idea that something can be true in itself, independent of its rhetorical, historical, **textual**, cultural and other forms of 'exteriority', is deeply imbricated in the idea that language originates with **speech** which is therefore more 'authentic' than **writing**. This 'phonocentric' belief in the absolute proximity of voice and thought makes it possible to conceive of truth in terms of an absolute or pure 'interiority'; or rather **phonocentrism** itself depends on the association of truth with the *logos* as the philosophical and theological **origin** of truth understood as self-revealing thought or cosmic reason. Hence logocentrism refers to 'the determination of the being of the entity as **presence**' (OG, 12). It refers to the idea that, before everything else (history, knowledge, consciousness, etc.), there is presence. Before everything, there is the Logos, the undeconstructible origin of the meaning of being, the rationality of thought, the absolute interiority of truth. Such things as history and knowledge, then, exist only 'as detours *for the purpose of* the reappropriation of presence' (OG, 10), for getting back to the Logos. In this way logocentrism is endemic to metaphysics in general and certainly dominates what 'philosophy' has been allowed to mean since Plato.

Platonic philosophy, as the very model of philosophy in the West, distinguishes between logic and rhetoric, relegating stylistic devices to the margins of a 'central' argument. In this way philosophy is opposed to text, since the purpose of philosophy lies in 'the reappropriation of presence' and the text exists only as an aid or **supplement** to that purpose. This constrains 'doing' philosophy to mean, as John D. Caputo puts it neatly, 'letting the logic lead the letter' (*Nutshell*, 83), or following the argument ahead of its representation on the presumption that philosophy is located **inside** the text, which is positioned on the **outside** of philosophy, the logos, truth and so on. In general, then, logocentrism designates any supposition of the absolute priority and 'non-exteriority' of truth as the 'undeconstructible' origin of difference understood as oppositional difference (logic opposed to rhetoric, speech opposed to writing, the sensible opposed to the intelligible, etc.). This is not to say it would be anti-logocentric, or counter-metaphysical, to install a tow bar on a Ford Mustang. But it would be logocentric to suppose that a Mustang contains or exudes an essence that is both pre-deconstructive and undeconstructible.

There is no doubt that, for a certain community, 'the' Mustang (which is to say Mustangs produced from 1964 to around 1968) does signify an essence – of industrial art, perhaps, the ultimate driving experience or the sexiest affordable car ever built. Whatever 'essence' the Mustang could be said to signify (and we've already listed several, which ought to complicate the idea of there being only one – and what is an essence that it might be multiple?), it will function as the standard against which deviations, imitations, corruptions, misuses, fabrications and the like are measured. 'And this', Derrida remarks (albeit without reference to Mustangs), 'is not just *one* metaphysical gesture among others, it is *the* metaphysical exigency, that which has been the most constant, most profound and most potent' (LI, 93). The gesture, which is inescapable within metaphysics, involves an assumption of the pre-deconstructive and undeconstructible essence or logos of a thing (the essence of philosophy, the essence of literature, the essence of being and so on) such that something else appears as secondary, supplementary or inessential (or as essentially other). Hence the essence of language is contained in speech, compared to which writing is a no doubt useful but nonetheless inessential technology for representing that essence; or the essence of philosophy resides in logic or reason, for which textual devices exist as useful but inessential technologies for communicating philosophical truths. Those devices (figures of speech, turns of phrase, the accoutrements of 'style', etc.) are never in any way philosophical in themselves and neither is philosophy 'itself' in any way textual.

None of this is meant to suggest that logocentrism constitutes a kind of 'wrong turn' in the history of thought, or that it should be easy to think against logocentrism. There's nothing wrong in attributing a certain value to the power and beauty of a Mustang, the poetic grandeur of *King Lear* or the philosophical significance of **Kant**. It's not as if, by doing **deconstruction**, one is forced to let go of the idea that some things are more valuable than others. The point is not to try to escape logocentrism, which would be impossible, but to try to show that every 'essence' is a *text*. This is a different way of looking at things. But the difference that proceeds from starting out with the view that there is nothing outside of the text, that the 'essential' value of a thing is an effect of con-textuality (**differance**, writing, the **trace**), does not point to relativism or social apathy. Deconstruction's difference may lie in putting differance before presence, but not – on the contrary – in order to avoid questions concerning **justice**, **responsibility** or **democracy**. In holding to the undecidability of things, the point of deconstruction may be that we need to find other ways than logocentrism provides us with for continuing to believe in and support the value of an idea such as justice or democracy. (See also HEIDEGGER, INTENTIONALITY, PLAY, PROPER, STRUCTURE.)

**mark**   Derrida often uses the term 'mark' instead of 'sign', because the latter harbours a certain ontology (or the **trace** of one) in the relationship of signifier and signified. The concept of the sign, even **Saussure**'s radical concept of the arbitrary **structure** of the sign, necessitates an idea of unity, of something that is fully constituted and **present** to itself. This runs counter to Saussure's own logic, which insists that no sign ever 'is' simply on its own: every sign is always the sign of something else – another sign. The sign's ontology, then, is very strange indeed: 'half of it always "not there"', as Gayatri Spivak remarks, 'and the other half always "not that"' ('Preface', p. xvii). If the sign may be said to open the question of **being**, it does so by opening 'being' to others (to the 'not there' and the 'not that' of being), or to the necessity of being *with* others ('being there' as 'being with'). And in this strange ontology the sign alone 'escapes the instituting question of philosophy: "What is . . . ?"' (OG, 19).

For all this, in so far as the signifier–signified relationship imparts a certain unity to the sign (albeit a divided one), the concept of the sign remains within the history of thought understood as the history of the **metaphysics** of presence. Such a history cannot think what must come *before* the sign, or before a system of ontological differences in the form, say, of the difference between signifier and signified, or sign and referent. And what comes before the sign Derrida sometimes calls a mark (but note that this is not an antonym of 'sign'). A mark, then, whether spoken, written, gestural, pictorial or otherwise, is the sign deconstructed of presence; it is the sign without the concept of the sign. It is what the sign must be in order for it to signify or mean. Before a word makes sense, for example, it is a mark – a black mark on a white page in the case of a written word. It has to be a mark in order to be a word. But once it becomes a word (comes into presence, as it were) it remains a mark; every word is always also a mark. This remainder or survival of the mark persists in every sign, as a trace of every sign's 'origin' prior to its **origin** within presence. What might be said to linger within presence, then, is this trace of an absence – an absence that presence must erase. 'The trace', Derrida writes, 'is not only the disappearance of origin – within the discourse that we sustain and according to the path that we follow it means that the origin did not even disappear, that it was never constituted except reciprocally by a nonorigin, the trace, which thus becomes the origin of the origin' (OG, 61). In this way, too, the non-originariness of the mark disturbs the idea that signs begin or end in presence. (See also DIFFERANCE, DISSEMINATION, ITERABILITY, PROPER, SPEECH–WRITING OPPOSITION, SPECTRALITY, UNDECIDABILITY.)

**messianism**    There was much discomfort among his fans when Dylan 'turned Christian' in the 1970s with the release of *Slow Train Coming*, and no doubt there are those today who wonder whether even Derrida hasn't found God now that he's started talking about the messianic. Looking back, the biblical word-plays and revivalist style of Dylan's songs from that time hardly seem to count as proof of a religious conversion on his part, and likewise there is nothing in *Specters of Marx*, for all its talk about the promise of a future to come, which might lead one to suppose that Derrida must have set off recently towards Damascus. What Derrida means by the messianic has got nothing to do with the coming of any Messiah with a proper name (Jesus Christ, for instance, or Godot), though it does have everything to do with coming – 'the coming of the other', as he puts it, 'the absolute and unpredictable singularity of the *arrivant as justice*' (SoM, 28).

Derrida's interest in the messianic is drawn from an essay by Walter Benjamin, 'Theses on the Philosophy of History' (written in the 1920s), in which Benjamin refers to a 'weak messianic power' that relates each of us today to those who came and suffered before us. We are the chosen ones, as it were, whose present time was once the promised future of the past, and it is our **responsibility** to remember and redress the injustices that were suffered by those who made it possible for us to live. For Derrida, this is to rethink the present in terms of a never-ending future to come, based on our 'inheritance' from the past. Take for instance our acceptance of the eight-hour working day as an industrial standard. This standard didn't come from out of the blue; those who are no longer with us struggled and suffered to achieve it. What we have inherited is not just the achievement of that standard, but also the suffering that produced it. Our inheritance (or the promise of a future to come) is a **gift** from others who could not have known us. Hence we have a sort of double responsibility: to give to others whom we cannot know the gift of time to come, and to continue to struggle in the present for the preservation and development of the achievements (like the eight-hour working day, or the concept of **democracy**) that others gave to us. This is why Derrida insists that inheritance always involves 'the work of mourning', calling us to remember the others of the past who promised us a future in which others (like us) could come 'to be' (the reference here, of course, is to Shakespeare's *Hamlet*). Our time today, then, is really 'out of joint' with history understood as **presence**, for every moment of the present day remains absolutely open to the **spectrality** of others – to *revenants* and *arrivants* who never quite take the form of 'historical subjects' with **proper** names.

Of what does our inheritance consist? It consists of *today*, the present, this very moment that was given to us – made possible – by the past. We must remember this, and mourn. But within this very moment there is the possibility – a messianic promise – of other moments to come. We must never let that promise take the form of a programmed future (by having to invade Iraq, for instance, or having to go to Mass on Sundays), since this would be to close ourselves off from what must be allowed to come unexpectedly. Derrida didn't learn this lesson of the messianic from reading the Bible; he learned it from reading Benjamin – and Karl Marx. 'We believe', he writes, 'that this messianic remains an *ineffaceable* **mark** – a mark one neither can nor should efface – of Marx's legacy, and doubtless of *inheriting*, of the experience of inheritance in general. Otherwise, one would reduce the event-ness of the **event**, the singularity and the alterity of the other' (SoM, 28). Marx's 'legacy', then, is irreducible to a programme or manifesto for change. What we have inherited from Marx – and in a sense what we've inherited from the Enlightenment – is not a programme for change, but rather the messianic promise of change.

Now it's clear that there is nothing very 'messianic' about the promise to invade Iraq, and so it follows that Derrida's insistence on the messianic promise of a future to come does not include a desire for more violence and injustice. On the contrary, Derrida's messianism – 'without content and without identifiable messiah' (SoM, 28) – is all about keeping the future open to the possibility of less violence and injustice, a possibility that rests on not allowing oneself to believe that the future must depend 'on the good conscience of having done one's duty' today (ibid.). In order to be responsible for and to the future (for and to democracy and justice), we cannot let ourselves be guided by a sense of duty as determined by present-day political, religious, moral or other programmes. Waiting for the Messiah with a proper name (whether it be Christ, Godot or the US-appointed successor to Saddam Hussein) won't change anything, because what one would be waiting for is the coming of an actual event (which of course might never happen, albeit that's neither here nor there). And actual events belong to the history of presence, to history *as* presence, even when they take the form of a spiritual promise. But Derrida's radical sense of an absolutely open future to come, a future that must always remain to come, necessitates an acceptance of having to wait – without waiting, without thinking to *know* what we're waiting for, without being conscious of waiting – for what he sometimes calls the 'absolute' event whose coming must be unexpected. What else is there to wait for? (See also DIFFERANCE, IDENTITY, METAPHYSICS, NEW INTERNATIONAL, SPEECH–WRITING OPPOSITION, YES.)

**metaphysics**   The idea that truth has an essence goes back to **Plato** and remains powerful today. It seems almost impossible to think anything at all without thinking that, both ultimately and from the start, 'the truth' of what you're thinking is independent of your thoughts. This is to say that our thinking requires us not to think of the 'essence' of truth as a question that needs to be thought through, but rather as the fundamental ground or necessary **origin** of thought in general. Following **Heidegger**, Derrida uses the term *metaphysics* to designate the history of this way of thinking, which is based on the 'priority' and 'exteriority' of truth. For Heidegger, though, metaphysics ends or culminates with **Nietzsche**, who 'reverses' metaphysics by giving priority to art over truth (see Nietzsche, *Will*). In this way the 'truth' of truth is to be found in aesthetic mystification rather than in philosophical or religious prescription, yet nonetheless Heidegger insists that 'Nietzsche does not pose the question of truth proper' (*Nietzsche*, 148), and so his thinking remains within the history of thought as metaphysics even while seeming to unsettle its most basic assumption. Briefly, Heidegger argues that Nietzsche fails to engage with the essence of truth *as a question*. Hence the reversal of metaphysics occurs within metaphysics, because Nietzsche continues to assume rather than to question the essence of truth or **being**.

The way out of metaphysics, on Heidegger's account, is to acknowledge that the truth or 'movement' of being involves the 'mystery' of absence. The **presence** of every being, in other words, necessitates a projection of itself towards an end that remains to come and is therefore absent. The being-present of an apprentice carpenter, say, involves the projection of that being towards a becoming in the form of a qualified tradesman or craftsman, just as the seed projects itself towards the plant. This is to rethink absence beyond its opposition to presence, or to think of absence as a kind of quasi-presence that is essential to being. It might even be to think of absence as a force that 'discloses' or 'dispenses' being, or which gives any being or entity a sense of its own presence or **identity**. But, Heidegger insists, in order to think this way, to think the 'way out' of metaphysics, it is necessary to go back to the origin of metaphysics, which is to be understood not so much in terms of a historical moment or location but as a structural possibility. And this entails what he calls 'a *destruction* – a critical process in which the traditional concepts, which at first must necessarily be employed, are de-constructed (*kritischer Abbau*) down to the sources from which they were drawn' (*Basic Problems*, 22–3).

The problem here, from Derrida's point of view, lies with the notion of deconstructing 'down', as though **deconstruction** stood for a process of disintegration or distillation down to some kind of primordial or pro-to-metaphysical essence which remains somehow hidden to metaphysics while functioning also to inaugurate it. In more general terms, Derrida parts company with Heidegger whenever the latter seems to invoke a notion of some lost or primordial place (the 'homeland') of Being, which can be thought only within the German language as the modern equivalent of ancient Greek. *That* Heidegger is, for Derrida, 'always horribly dangerous and wildly funny, certainly grave and a bit comical' (OS, 68). But in any case the point is that Derrida sees Heidegger's project of the 'destruction' of metaphysics as a familiar attempt to produce a clearer or 'truer' picture of essences; hence for Derrida 'the destruction of metaphysics remains within metaphysics, only making explicit its principles' (MoP, 48). In one sense, that is, the whole point of the destruction of metaphysics is to 'let be' the singularities of beings-in-particular. It is precisely the singularity or the 'there-being' of every being-in-particular (or *Dasein*) that a gener-alizing metaphysics cannot see, because its sights are set on understanding the nature of (human) being-in-general. This is what justifies the destruc-tion of metaphysics. Yet despite Heidegger's best efforts to lead us out of metaphysics (within which the truth of each being's experience of his or her singularity is concealed under the general heading of 'human nature'), it would appear that, once the way 'outside' of metaphysics has been found, all beings arrive at being joined or 'gathered' together as one (again) in their knowledge of the unity of Being and truth.

The point is taken up by Derrida in *Specters of Marx*, where he criticizes Heidegger's notion of the 'harmonious accord' between beings determined by the rule of *dike* (as Heidegger interprets the famous Anaximander fragment), which allocates to every being its '**proper**' time and place (see Heidegger, *Early Greek*). The notion that every being is held in some kind of unity or togetherness with other beings, each of which has been assigned its place in the world by the non-moral, non-legal asystematic 'system' of *dike* (as **justice**) remains for Derrida an inextricably metaphysical notion. So for example I might well be 'gathered up' in some kind of a relation to someone who thought that Geri Halliwell's version of 'It's Raining Men' (2001) is a great record; but that would be to invoke an incredibly loose if not effectively meaningless sense of 'gathering'. This would not be to say that fans of The Weather Girls (whose original recording of the song, in 1982, is as 'fat' as Geri Halliwell's version is 'anorexic') must constitute a unified 'gathering' of beings conjoined in their mutual disregard for the musical mis-hits of the former 'Ginger Spice'. Or as Derrida puts it, possibly without ever having heard of the Spice Girls, Heidegger's 'mythology' of the gathering of beings overlooks the question of justice, which depends on 'the irreducible excess of a disjointure or an anachrony'. It depends not on actual differences in themselves, as it were, but on **differance** as a **structure** that 'would alone be able to *do justice* or to *render justice* to the other as other' (SoM, 27).

Deconstruction is opposed to anything that claims to gather up, to unite, to bring together as one – whether in the form of an 'accord' within Being or as the 'spirit' of a nation. For whatever gathers up also closes off. To gather all of us together in the here and now, for example, would be to close us off from the others who are no longer living and the others who are not yet living. Any gathering of beings (or the gathering of Being) – in the guise of a nation, perhaps, a rave party or a Bruce Springsteen concert – makes sense only as a gathering of beings in their presence, in the present time, in accordance with the metaphysics of Being as presence. Such a gathering cannot admit the ghosts of the past (*specters*) and the others yet to come (*arrivants*) – it cannot respond to the other's radical otherness because it continues to confine 'being' to the opposition of presence and absence, accordance and discordance, juncture and disjuncture and so on. This metaphysics has no place for Derrida's radical (if not impossible) sense of a justice beyond calculation, outside the law, in excess of rights and a notion of what is proper. The metaphysics of presence has no time for ghosts (for a 'community' of spectres), for the others who do not belong to the communal gathering of present-beings who fit an ideal of the proper subject. (See also DEMOCRACY, EVENT, LOGOCENTRISM, MESSIANISM, NEW INTERNATIONAL, PHONOCENTRISM, POSTAL METAPHOR, SPECTRALITY, SPEECH–WRITING OPPOSITION.)

**new international**   As I write, the 'most unpopular war in history' is being waged by a 'coalition of the willing', led by the United States and not the United Nations, against a country that has not been convicted of any crimes under international law. But of course this is not how the 'coalition' sees it. The publicly stated justification, which has failed to win public consent, for bringing terror to Baghdad is given as Iraq's 'non-compliance' with a longstanding UN order to disarm. Despite failing to win public support or UN approval, then, the invasion of Iraq turns out to depend for its justification on being seen to have international backing. The argument goes something like this: a certain interpretation (one that might be called self-serving, duplicitous or false) of UN Resolution 1441 authorizes military action against Iraq in the event of its refusal to disarm. But the 'problem' is that the United Nations – representing an international coalition of nation states – has shown itself to be unwilling to invoke the terms of its own charter, a charter vested with the authority of international law. Hence the necessity to form a 'new international' – the Coalition of the Willing – in the name of making 'tough' decisions on behalf of global peace.

Under the banner of an international alliance – albeit an unelected, unofficial confederation within which only the United States wields any international force or influence – universal **responsibility** takes the place of national self-interest. But what 'universal' means according to this usage is limited (as Derrida remarked shortly after the last time there was an 'international' declaration of war on Iraq) to the interests of a certain ideal of liberal **democracy** as defined, in real-political terms, not by the United Nations of the World but by the United States of America.

For it must be cried out, at a time [in the early 1990s] when some have the audacity to neo-evangelize in the name of the ideal of a liberal democracy that has finally realized itself as the ideal of human history: never have violence, inequality, exclusion, famine, and thus economic oppression affected as many human beings in the history of the earth and of humanity. (SoM, 85)

In this context, how have the interests of universal responsibility been served by the internationally sanctioned trade embargoes against Iraq since the first Gulf War? Which of the nations among the Coalition of the Willing would be prepared to take responsibility for the economic oppression, let alone the medically preventible deaths of thousands of Iraqi civilians, caused by those embargoes? Which of those nations would be willing to take responsibility for having forgotten until now to do anything to prevent Iraq's well-documented persecution of the Kurds? Which of them will stand accountable for having forgotten, too, that Saddam Hussein, when his troops were on the side of 'freedom' against the anti-modern theocracy in Iran or the Soviet-backed communists in Afghanistan in the 1980s, was supported by (among others) the United States – to whose good conscience today's New International is indebted?

There was another Bush in the White House when Derrida was pointing out (in *Specters of Marx*) the signs of an emerging 'new international' of global corporations, powerful nation states and criminal organizations forming around the 'triumph of liberal democracy' after the collapse of the USSR. At that time the 'new international' never spoke its name although it did have a best-selling manifesto in the form of Francis Fukuyama's *The End of History and the Last Man* (1992), a book which goes to great lengths to make the ideology of the 'new world order' seem anything but ideological. Derrida could not have foreseen back then, of course, that the Coalition of the Willing would become the semi-official (if no doubt provisional) name of the emerging 'new international' he was describing after Gulf War I. Yet should that Coalition be disbanded in the near future, this will not mean that the 'new international' will have disappeared but only that it will have receded from public view. For the point is that the 'new international' dare not speak its name except when a certain kind of **event**, in the form of a so-called crisis of international law, presents it with an opportunity to defend 'freedom' by opposing 'tyranny'. In this way the interests of nation states (though not only these) are concealed under the higher purpose of an 'international' cause. The violation of 'human rights' in Iraq, then, is an offence to international **justice** and constitutes a crisis of international law to the extent that the oppressions of the Iraqi regime have been allowed to go unchecked and unpunished. Within these terms the 'new international' gives itself an unimpeachable universal responsibility for going to war on behalf of liberating others. But against a background of recent history this 'universal' responsibility seems to be highly selective and anything but universal, raising the question of what an event has to be in order to be seen as a 'crisis' demanding an international response. No one seems to feel any universal responsibility to organize a 'coalition of the willing' into a war with Russia, for example, whose brutal mistreatment of its Chechen population could (and surely should) be interpreted as an offence to international justice. Why is this not seen as an event? Why isn't it seen as a crisis of international law? And why didn't the USA or any other nation feel compelled to liberate 'the others' of Chile under the Pinochet regime, when thousands of Chilean civilians were tortured and murdered in the wake of a military coup on another September 11, this time in 1973? (No, the calendar does not belong to any nation.) Or what happened to the expression of a universal responsibility to uphold human rights when it came to the psychotic crimes of Pol Pot's US-friendly Khmer Rouge in a Cambodia where millions of civilians were killed, in the 1970s, at the hands of their own government? Where were the coalitions of the willing when those other others in Indonesia under Suharto, say, or in Nicaragua under Somosa's dictatorship, could have done with a bit of international support?

'A "new international" is being sought', as Derrida put it long before the invasion of Iraq, 'through these crises of international law' (SoM, 85), albeit what it means for an event to count as a 'crisis' would appear to be open to much interpretation. Under the guise of universal responsibility, the rhetoric of the 'new international' reveals itself to be a sham. For even back then, over a decade ago, Derrida could write that 'it already denounces the limits of a discourse on human rights that will remain inadequate, sometimes hypocritical, and in any case formalistic and inconsistent with itself as long as the law of the market, the "foreign debt," the inequality of techno-scientific, military, and economic development maintain an effective inequality as monstrous as that which prevails today, to a greater extent than ever in the history of humanity' (ibid.).

There can be no question that Derrida owes his criticism of the 'new international' to Marx. In his own words, 'one may still find inspiration in the Marxist "spirit" to criticize the presumed autonomy of the juridicial and to denounce endlessly the *de facto* take-over of international authorities by powerful Nation-States, by concentrations of techno-scientific capital, symbolic capital, and financial capital, of State capital and private capital' (ibid.). But he also draws from this Marxist 'spirit' the inspiration to speculate on the emergence of another possible form of the 'new international', which he calls 'a link of affinity, suffering, and hope' (ibid.). This would be 'an alliance without institution', and 'we have more than one sign of it' today (ibid.). Again, Derrida was writing before '9/11', before the 'war on terror', before the 'pre-emptive strike' against Iraq. Surely, though, the many forms of worldwide 'unofficial' resistance – popular, academic and political resistance and so on – to 'official' justifications for the war, shed some light on Derrida's notion of this other 'new international'. Consider, for example, all those massive public demonstrations in cities around the world: where's the party, the institution or the leader responsible for organizing them? Aren't these demonstrations, then, one of the signs of 'an alliance without institution' – 'without coordination, without party, without country, without national community (International before, across, and beyond any national determination), without co-citizenship, without common belonging to a class' (ibid.)? What, moreover, is the organizing force behind all the political satire on the Internet – all those satiric images, the audio files, the jokes (Interviewer: But how do you *know* they've got weapons of mass destruction? Pentagon official: We've kept all the receipts.), the cartoons, the quick-time videos and so on, not to mention all the sites listing the Bush family's history of business dealings with the Saudis (especially the bin Ladens) and the on-line commentaries by the likes of Gore Vidal and Norman Mailer: who's responsible for all *that*?

So for Derrida there are two 'new internationals' – opposing forces or spirits, as it were – and it's clear to which of these he extends his approval. But we should be careful not to think that Derrida is advocating a kind of naïve populism here. What might be called the spiritually Marxist form of the new international should not be mistaken for an alliance ('without institution') based on sentimentality, though no doubt there are good sentimental reasons for wanting to oppose 'the *de facto* take-over of international authorities' and for feeling dubious about the need for any war. After all, as 'a link of affinity, suffering, and hope', this other new international cannot be said to exclude a certain sentimentality as a necessary condition of 'belonging'. What must not be overlooked, however, is Derrida's insistence on the link to *Marx*, who founded (in 1864) the First International, 'The International Working Men's Association'. This doesn't mean that all the criticism, analysis and documentary evidence on the Internet, and all the rallies around the world, should be understood as conscious or even unconscious manifestations of 'Marxism'. This other new international is not reducible to a 'people's movement' and neither is it formally or informally 'communist'. But still Derrida insists that this 'alliance without institution' (or without **presence**) is linked to a certain Marxist spirit. All those who might belong (without belonging) to it, then, are in debt to Marx, 'even if they no longer believe or never believed in the socialist-Marxist International, in the dictatorship of the proletariat, in the messiano-eschatalogical role of the universal union of the proletariat of all lands' (SoM, 86). The crucial condition is not belief or consciousness, in other words, but inspiration: those who might be called associates of the new international 'continue to be inspired by at least one of the spirits of Marx or Marxism' (ibid.). Without that inspiration there would be no 'link of affinity, suffering, and hope', and hence the only socio-political alternatives would remain as they are at present (a party-politics of the left or a party-politics of the right, a culture of the East or a culture of the West, an internationalism of the United Nations or an internationalism of the Coalition of the Willing, etc.).

In a word, the link to Marx keeps the link of 'affinity, suffering, and hope' from falling back into pure sentimentality or vulgar populism. This other 'new internationalism' thus holds open the possibility of radical critique. 'With us', as Marx proclaimed to a meeting of the Communist League in 1850, 'it is not a matter of reforming private property, but of abolishing it; not of hushing up the class antagonism, but of abolishing the classes; not of ameliorating the existing society, but of establishing a new one' ('Address', 64). Those who would belong to this 'conjuration' (which is not the same) today, Derrida insists, continue to draw inspiration from Marx

> in order to ally themselves, in a new, concrete, and real way, even if this alliance no longer takes the form of a party or of a workers' international, but rather of a kind of counter-conjuration, in the (theoretical and practical) critique of the state of international law, the concepts of State and nation, and so forth: in order to renew this critique, and especially to radicalize it. (SoM, 86)

Such is the link that must be maintained to a politics of revolution, even and especially if the revolution has to occur within the very concept of politics 'itself'. *This* new international, a continuation (by other means) of Marx's radical inspiration for change, cannot be dismissed as 'sentimental'. Without it – on the contrary – nothing today would be left. (See also ARTIFACTUALITY, IDENTITY, MESSIANISM, SPECTRALITY, UNDECIDABILITY, VIRTUALITY, YES.)

**Nietzsche, Friedrich** (German philosopher, 1844–1900)   Just about anything you might want to say about Nietzsche could, circumstances considered, count as true. It's no accident that Nietzsche's writing is often accused of anti-semitism, misogyny, proto-Nazism, nihilism, hedonism, misanthropy, unbounded pessimism, immorality, scornful atheism and the like – as though it were all just so much sound and fury signifying nothing more than the bilious ramblings of a deeply troubled mind, and a body racked with syphilitic pain. Equally, it's not uncommon to find his writing praised for its astonishing affirmation of the energy and tragedy of life, the purity of joy, the awful truth of alienation or the creative power of difference. As a philosopher, Nietzsche cuts a very scandalous figure indeed.

And this of course is why Derrida is drawn to him. It is not that Derrida sides either way on the is-he-or-isn't-he question of whether Nietzsche was a misogynist, a fascist, a madman, etc. What interests him instead is the **undecidability** of that question, on the one hand, and on the other that the question is put to Nietzsche's writing but not usually to that of other philosophers (albeit **Heidegger** poses a certain kind of exception here). What might be at stake, then, is not so much the issue of Nietzsche 'himself' but the question of Nietzsche's *writing*, or the question of **writing** generally and the status of philosophy with regards to a certain idea of writing. As the most 'literary' (rhetorical, stylish, figural) example of philosophical discourse, Nietzsche's writing may be said to over-play the representational (the **textual**) at the expense of the philosophical. In a word, rhetoric comes before dialectic in Nietzsche – or this is how his writing can be read. Precisely because it is open to be read, his writing is subject to interpretation and misinterpretation, accusation and counter-accusation and so on. But the 'scandal' that Nietzsche's writing may be said to open is not reducible to that writing since, on Derrida's account, it opens a scandal within philosophy. No matter how much philosophy may try to suppress its textuality, in other words, it can never avoid being 'a kind of writing' (as argued famously by Richard Rorty). In Nietzsche, the **supplementary** relations between philosophy and writing loom inescapably large. But the point is that while clearly this counts as an individual performance or a particular style, it is also an instance of a general **structure** that not even the most rigorously logical, rational or reasoned philosophical text could hope to defeat or master. References to Nietzsche abound in Derrida's work, but see *Spurs* and *The Ear of the Other* for sustained discussions. (See also DIFFERANCE, ITERABILITY, LOGOCENTRISM, METAPHYSICS, PLATO, SPEECH–WRITING OPPOSITION.)

**origin** Within **metaphysics**, every origin is thought in terms of '**presence without difference**' (OG, 215) – an ideal moment of pure, unmediated 'firstness', as it were. **Speech** comes before **writing**, nature before culture, **being** before beings and so on, according to a logic that positions writing, culture and beings in a relation of 'secondariness' to an original state or condition. This relation is both oppositional and hierarchical, with secondariness understood as a fall or lapse from firstness.

Derrida uses the expression 'presence without difference' to designate what he sees as Rousseau's ideal of the origin in the latter's attempt to account for the origin of language. The contextual occasion of Derrida's remarks should not be overlooked, but all the same they can be taken for his general view on the metaphysical concept of the origin as presence-without-difference. What interests Derrida about the logic of Rousseau's *Essay on the Origin of Languages* (published in the mid-eighteenth century) is its reliance on 'the strange association of the values of effacement and substitution' (OG, 215), a reliance that Rousseau never quite acknowledges but of which he is not entirely unaware.

Rousseau argues that all human languages originate from the simple expression of passions. This origin persists in speech, which is 'natural language', compared to which the grammatical sophistication and con-ceptual complexity of writing are seen to have led us further and further into the realm of abstract thought and away from authentic social living. Rousseau makes the same case for music, whose 'natural' form is melody and against which harmonic sophistication must be seen as secondary and threatening. But what exactly is put at risk here, by writing and harmony, if not also by a certain notion of complexity that we might associate with advances in technology? Perhaps it is the anti-modern politics of Rousseau's nostalgic need to believe in the lost actuality of an authentic, pre-modern 'once upon a time' that has to be protected. The point is that Rousseau's defence of the origin as 'presence without difference' is not reducible simply to a philosophical argument, or more generally it is that the very concept of origin-as-presence belongs not only to philosophy; it permeates thought and therefore generates ethico-political decisions. Or rather it separates the making of a decision from the **responsibility** of having to decide, because nothing needs to be decided when it comes to choosing between the purity of an original and the impurity of an imitation.

Yet it turns out that the 'pure' firstness of speech and melody is not pure at all. For after asserting that speech and song 'were formerly one' Rousseau adds that this does not mean 'they were initially the same thing'; it means that '*both had the same source*' (cited in OG, 214). As Derrida notes, 'instead of concluding from this simultaneity that the song broached itself in grammar, that difference had already begun to corrupt melody, to make both it and its laws possible at the same time, Rousseau prefers to believe that grammar *must (should) have* been comprised, in the sense of being confused with, within melody. There *must (should) have* been plenitude and not lack, presence without difference' (OG, 215). The origin behind (as it were) the origin of speech and song must have been from the beginning divided from within. The origin of the origin is constituted by a breach within 'itself'. Firstness, then, *is* this breach or broach, which comes both before firstness and is the basis on which a concept of the purity of firstness (the absolute firstness of firstness) is possible. Firstness, in other words, begins in its difference from itself, and not in its difference from secondariness; from the start it already comes second. **Differance**, and not presence, is originary.

So for Derrida there is no origin except originary difference, which is what Rousseau was able to 'say without saying' (ibid.). Rousseau's whole argument is committed to warding off the dangers of **supplementarity**, but if speech and melody are indeed pure presences then why the constant need to define them against their secondary others in the form of writing and harmony? 'This conforms to the logic of **identity**', as Derrida puts it, 'and to the principle of classical ontology (the outside is outside, being is, etc.)' (ibid.). But if for instance the identity of speech depends on its difference from writing, what would it mean to say that speech 'itself' has an identity or presence of its own? Doesn't its identity begin in its difference from itself? Doesn't it begin in the non-oppositional order of

**inside–outside** relations? Doesn't it begin in what Derrida calls 'the logic of supplementarity, which would have it that the outside be inside, that the other and the lack come to add themselves as a plus that replaces a minus, that what adds itself to something takes the place of a default in the thing, that the default, as the outside of the inside, should be already within the inside, etc.' (ibid.)? It is in order to keep intact his concept of the origin as presence-without-difference that Rousseau is committed to oppose the logic of supplementarity, committing him to regard substitution in terms only of secondariness or copying. But to acknowledge the 'originality' of originary difference is to acknowledge that 'substitution has always already begun; that imitation, principle of art, has always already interrupted natural plenitude; that, having to be a *discourse*, it has always already broached presence in differance; that in Nature it [substitution] is always that which supplies Nature's lack, a voice that is substituted for the voice of Nature' (ibid.). There could be no concept of the origin as presence-without-difference in the absence of the work of supplementarity, substitution or so-called secondariness.

Everything begins then in representation, *as* representation, and can never leave this behind. But since representation belongs to 'the logic of identity' or 'the principle of classical ontology' as the perfect exemplar of secondariness – representation is always re-presentation of a presence that comes first – Derrida prefers not to say that there is nothing outside of representation, but that '*there is nothing outside of the* **text** [there is no outside-text; *il n'y a pas de hors-texte*]' (OG, 158). We can say here that what this means is that there is nothing outside originary difference or the work of supplementarity, nothing outside 'the absence of the referent or the transcendental signified' (ibid.). There is no pure origin or identity outside 'the strange association of the values of effacement and substitution'. (See also DISSEMINATION, ITERABILITY, LOGOCENTRISM, *PHARMAKON*, PHONOCENTRISM, TRACE, UNDECIDABILITY, VIRTUALITY.)

***pharmakon*** In a long and detailed reading of **Plato**'s *Phaedrus*, Derrida's attention is drawn to Plato's use of the Greek word *pharmakon* whose several meanings range (seemingly impossibly) from 'poison' to 'remedy' or 'cure'. How could a word or concept contain or hold within itself such opposing senses? Far from confronting this question (and so avoiding the question of **undecidability**), translators of the *Phaedrus* have traditionally resolved the 'impossibility' of the *pharmakon* by deciding which sense is appropriate (or **proper**) in the context of a given passage or according to Plato's intention. There is nothing unusual about this logic, which is used routinely to decide questions of interpretation on the basis that contextuality and **intentionality** determine meaning. But what happens when interpretations differ or when meanings can be shown to exceed the limits of any given context or an author's intentions? Surely this suggests that contextuality and intentionality are themselves products – not sources – of interpretation. No doubt Plato was aware of what he meant to say on every occasion that he used the word *pharmakon* and could see the links between its various meanings. Without denying that Plato had intentions and was able to see that *pharmakon* had multiple (even opposing) senses, should it be supposed that *pharmakon* is reducible to someone's interpretation of what Plato might have seen and therefore (supposedly) meant to say? Yes, there is a case for conceding that Plato sees the links within the word *pharmakon*. 'Then again', as Derrida puts it, 'in other cases, Plato can *not* see the links, can leave them in the shadow or break them up. And yet these links go on working of themselves. In spite of him? thanks to him? in *his* **text**? *outside* his text? but then where? between his text and the language? for what reader? at what moment?' (D, 96).

These are questions that may be answered on the assumption only that the complex signification of the word *pharmakon* (though of course not only this word) constitutes a system whose rules precede any act of interpretation. Signification comes before interpretation, then. What this logic (which applies not only to translation but also to criticism and understanding in general) presupposes is the absolute priority of truth to exposition, **presence** to representation, intention to reception and so on. In this it mirrors the **metaphysical** order of succession from **speech** to **writing**, which is precisely what the *pharmakon* is meant to illustrate despite serving to show, on Derrida's reading, only the opposite of what it is used to mean-to-say or to prove. 'No absolute privilege', Derrida argues, 'allows us absolutely to master its [the *pharmakon*'s] textual system' (D, 96). This is because the *pharmakon* is not a figure that clarifies the difference between speech and writing, as Plato intends, but functions on the contrary to illustrate that such a difference is always unsustainable. What is meant to sustain it, though, is a way of thinking that sees the priority of speech to and over writing as natural. In Plato's version of this **phonocentrism**, the *pharmakon* of writing refers to the presumption that written words must always be either 'good' or 'bad' ('poisonous' or 'remedial') to the extent that they are 'true' or 'false' according to how faithfully they represent spoken words. The founding assumption therefore is that speech comes before writing, which is to say that writing is always positioned as the **supplement** of (undeconstructible) speech.

The problem though is that the *pharmakon* does not work to guarantee this 'natural' or standard opposition between speech and writing. Instead, through its 'ambivalence', the *pharmakon* 'constitutes the medium in which opposites are opposed, the movement and the **play** that links them among themselves, reverses them or makes one side cross over into the other (soul/body, good/evil, **inside/outside**, memory/forgetfulness, speech/writing, etc.)' (D, 127). So, for example, one might say that the *pharmakon* of writing aids human memory by providing a record of something that truly happened or was said at a certain time and place; this would be writing as a 'good' *pharmakon* that 'cures' forgetfulness. But it could just as easily be said that writing is an 'evil' *pharmakon* that 'poisons' memory by replacing it with a simulacrum. Derrida's argument is not that the difference between the curative and the poisonous *pharmakon* precedes the difference between good and bad writing. On the contrary, his argument is that the *pharmakon* is the condition on which the opposition between remedy and poison, good and evil, speech and writing and so on is produced. As the movement and the play of 'ambiguity' at work, the *pharmakon* comes first; opposites come afterwards. Hence the *pharmakon* is 'the **differance** of difference' (D, 127); it is what must always 'precede', must always come 'before', any oppositional difference. Take the opposition between memory and forgetfulness: while this seems to describe a natural or foundational difference, it turns out to depend on something even more 'foundational' still, albeit which is insubstantial (or **spectral**) at the same time. For memory is always finite, as Plato acknowledges by 'attributing life to it' (D, 109). In its finitude, 'living' memory always has its limits. Indeed, as Derrida points out, memory-without-limit would not be memory at all; it would be 'infinite self-presence' (ibid.). Now, because memory is always limited, it 'always therefore already needs signs in order to recall the non-present, with which it is necessarily in relation' (ibid.). The opposition of self-present memory and non-self-present forgetfulness, then, must come after the *pharmakon* of writing as a system of signs that supplements, to good or bad effect, the truth of living memory or the authenticity of speech. Poison, illness, contamination – these always belong to memory at the start. Whether as the *pharmakon* or the supplement, writing does not threaten to contaminate memory from the outside. By its very nature, memory depends on substituting signs for presence and so is 'contaminated' from the beginning, before the opposition of inside and outside, speech and writing, etc. So to posit (as Plato does) a memory that is pure unto itself, completely independent of signs or supplementarity, would really be to dream of a memory that was something other than itself, a memory without writing (D, 109). This – the dream of infinite self-presence – conjures up not only an ideal of 'pure' memory but also, of course, that of 'pure' speech. In both cases, 'purity' and 'originality' are assigned to what comes 'before' the *pharmakon* of writing as the condition, paradoxically, by which purity and originality are able to be opposed to writing. To dream of infinite self-presence is, in other words, to write. (See also APORIA, HYMEN, IDENTITY, ITERABILITY, *KHORA*, LOGOCENTRISM, TEXT.)

**phonocentrism**     According to a powerful illusion, the phonetic sign is a 'sign' only in the most formal or strictest sense. When we are speaking, we don't usually feel we are using signs. We feel instead that we are expressing ourselves directly, as if there were an indissociable bond between what we say and what we think. This is not, as Derrida notes, 'merely one illusion among many'. Going all the way back to **Plato** at least, 'it is the condition of the very idea of truth' (OG, 20). Now this doesn't mean that Derrida doesn't believe in truth, or that **deconstruction** says that anything goes. It means that 'the very idea of truth' depends on truth being seen to stand alone, before and outside any means of representing it. Truth is over there, signs are over here. This idea isn't 'wrong', but it *is* an idea. It's a particular take on what truth means, giving us a particular idea of the world, for example, as distinguished from what we think of as other-worldly. So our idea of the world, which depends on 'the very idea of truth', separates the worldly and the other-worldly according to what is **inside** and **outside** our idea of 'the world'. This gives us the difference between people and ghosts, which Derrida puts into question through the logic of **spectrality**.

Now, what does the illusion consist of? It consists of 'the absolute effacement of the signifier' (OG, 20). This is what Derrida means by *phonocentrism* – the powerful idea that there is a difference between spoken words and written signs, with all the privilege being on the side of the former. Our 'experience of the effacement of the signifier in the voice' (ibid.) allows us to think that truth (signifieds, concepts, thought, etc.) can exist without mediation. On the basis of this experience, which is a real illusion, truth is understood to be outside the sign, outside appearances and forms. In speaking, then, we get 'the unique experience of the signified producing itself spontaneously, from within the self, and nevertheless, as signified concept, in the element of ideality or universality' (ibid.). It's as if, when we're speaking, we are producing signifieds for the first time and, at the same time, giving voice to signifieds that are not ours alone but belong in general to the realm of truth, 'in the element of ideality and universality'. Even **Saussure** himself took this to be true, claiming that 'the natural bond' – 'the only true bond' – of signifier and signified occurs in *sound* (cited in OG, 35). Like so many others before him and since, Saussure looked on **writing** as a secondary and artificial system of com-munication, albeit it's the one he puts forward repeatedly as the very model for his theory of language as a system of differences '*without positive terms*' (*Course*, 120). What Saussure's phonocentrism (which is **metaphysics**) prevented him from seeing, though, is that the differential relations he attributes to writing must always already have been in place before speech could become a system of communication. Had he been less phonocentric, Derrida maintains, Saussure's radical theory of the sign would have led him to see writing as the general field of differential relations by and in which we think and communicate. Saussure's theory of the sign, then, opens not the possibility of a general semiotics, but a general *grammatology* as the name of 'a vast field' which accepts the written sign or inscription (the *gram*) as typical of signs in general according to Saussure's own thesis of 'the arbitrariness of the sign' (OG, 51). (See also DIFFERANCE, ITERABILITY, LOGOCENTRISM, SPEECH–WRITING OPPOSITION, STRUCTURE, SUPPLEMENTARITY.)

**Plato** (Greek philosopher, *c*.427–347 BC)    If philosophy has a **proper** method and a proper object, these could be said to derive from Plato. That's not to infer that every philosopher since Plato has speculated on the same object, or that every philosophical speculation conforms to the principles of an unvarying method. But what would philosophy mean if it did not have a sense of something that was 'proper' to itself? And of course for 'philosophy' we could substitute any number of other terms. Clearly the hoary question of what exactly it is that is proper to philosophy could lead to endless contemplation; so let's just say here that, for a **text** to be understood as philosophical, the minimum requirement is that the 'philosophy' part of the text is not itself seen to be textual. The philosophy part can be taken 'out' of the text, without causing any damage to that part. So for example **Kant** could be said to have written his *Critique of Judgement* in order that others might grasp what he was on about. Once you've 'got' Kant, you don't have to read him again. Indeed you only ever 'read' philosophy for the same reason that a chicken crosses the road – to get to the other side, which, in philosophy's case, amounts to the *inside* of the text. That's where philosophy is, and that's why it can be taken out of the text altogether.

On the basis of this **inside–outside** distinction it is possible to conceive of philosophy, as Derrida remarks of Hegel's philosophy (or Hegel's 'Platonism', as it were), as a discourse on 'the meaning of thought in the act of thinking itself and producing itself in the element of universality' (D, 10). For philosophy since Plato, then, questions concerning style and form are subordinate to questions concerning method and content. So it isn't that a book like Ray Monk's biography of Wittgenstein, written in a style to die for, is not quite a philosophical text because it's so stylish. It's not quite philosophical in itself because it doesn't quite 'contain' enough philosophical 'content'. And of course it's true that there must be something like a content which is (in a sense) proper to philosophy, or properly philosophical. Derrida's complaint with Platonism does not deny this point. His complaint has to do rather with the fact that in order to tie philosophy down to a notion of uncontextual truth or content, anything and everything else that philosophy could mean and do has to be suppressed. For some of Derrida's extended encounters with the text of Plato's philosophy, see especially *Dissemination, The Post-Card* and *On the Name*. (See also LOGOCENTRISM, METAPHYSICS, NIETZSCHE, *PHARMAKON*, PHONOCENTRISM, SPEECH–WRITING OPPOSITION, SUPPLEMENTARITY.)

**play**  When Derrida writes about 'play', he doesn't mean 'freeplay' or wanton 'playfulness'. He doesn't mean, 'playing around with – for the heck of it'. Although he seldom uses the term these days, 'play' appears frequently in some of Derrida's earlier work, especially of course in the 1967 essay '**Structure**, Sign, and Play in the Discourse of the Human Sciences'. In that essay and elsewhere he makes it clear that 'play' means something like 'give' or 'tolerance' (the tolerance within a finely tuned engine, for example, or the give in a taut length of rope), which works against ideas of self-sufficiency and absolute completion. Far from being grounded in **presence**, then, the **identity** of a thing is grounded without being grounded in this possibility of play – the internal play (or plays) of the movement of **supplementarity**. 'Play is the disruption of presence', as Derrida puts it (WD, 292). This means that in order for anything to be understood in terms of presence (to be self-sufficient, say), what has to be overlooked is its inscription within 'a system of differences and the movement of a chain' – a chain or series of 'signifying and substitutive' **marks** (ibid.). This system is the play of presences and absences. To understand the word 'cat', for example, in terms of presence or self-sufficiency, what has to be overlooked is the structurally necessary and signifying absence of the words 'bat', 'fat', 'sat', etc. Without such absence, there could be no presence. 'Play is always play of absence and presence', Derrida writes, 'but if it is to be thought radically, play must be conceived of before the alternative of presence and absence' (ibid.). Before there is presence or absence, in other words, there is play. There is always already some play or movement – a little give or tolerance – within the opposition of presence and absence, such that the opposition depends on this play as the condition of its possibility. '**Being** must be conceived as presence or absence', as Derrida remarks by way of an example, 'on the basis of the possibility of play and not the other way around' (ibid.).

In the 1970s and 1980s, however, a certain stand of what Christopher Norris calls 'deconstruction on the wild side' took hold among some US literary critics, based on a misinterpretation of Derrida's 'play' as 'freeplay' or a kind of quasi-Nietzschean 'creativity' (see Norris, *Deconstruction*, 90–125). 'Greatly overestimated in my texts in the United States,' Derrida says himself, 'this notion of "freeplay" is an inadequate translation of the lexical network connected to the word *jeu*, which I used in my first texts, but sparingly and in a highly defined manner' (LI, 115–16). The manner he refers to is the sense in which 'play' means the 'play of absence and presence' that must come before, in a quasi-transcendental fashion, any opposition of absence and presence. (See also DIFFERANCE, HYMEN, ITERABILITY, *KHORA*, *PHARMAKON*, POSTAL METAPHOR, SPEECH–WRITING OPPOSITION, TRACE, UNDECIDABILITY.)

**postal metaphor**    In its ideal form, a postal system guarantees that letters will arrive safely at their intended addresses. Yet everyone (including the postmaster general) knows that this does not always happen. Every time you post a letter, any one of three things can happen next: it will arrive where you intended it to be sent; it will arrive somewhere else (at another address, which might be the dead letter office); or it will never arrive, having been lost in the post. It's true that, more often than not, letters do arrive at the addresses we send them to, but no postal system can prevent the **structural** possibility of any letter going astray. Paradoxically, then, a letter's arrival depends on the structural possibility of its non-arrival. Without the possibility that every letter may not arrive, no letter could be said to arrive as intended. From this it transpires that arrival is a special type of non-arrival, such that a letter 'arrives' only by an 'accident' of the post. No letter can be guaranteed a smooth passage from signatory to addressee, and so every arrival is always in some sense accidental.

Certainly no force of intention on the part of a signatory can guarantee that a letter will be delivered to its correct address. **Intentionality** offers no protection against postal mishaps, which are in fact the very condition on which it is possible for a postal system to be seen as running smoothly (most of the time). A postal system can minimize but never eliminate mailing accidents; without them, it wouldn't be possible for a postal system to be in good working order.

To rethink the nature of a postal system in terms of the necessity of non-arrival entails a rethinking of the concept of arrival or destination in general. Hence the postal 'metaphor' is not quite metaphorical in the sense of being a representation of something other than itself. The dependence of a letter's arrival on the possibility of its non-arrival constitutes a particular form of a general condition, but this is not to suppose that the structural necessity of non-arrival pertaining to the postal system is a 'vehicle' for expressing an independent and pre-existing 'tenor'. The structural necessity of non-arrival conditions every system of communication, from **speech** to **writing** (in the standard sense) and beyond. To this extent the postal metaphor (or the postal condition, necessity or effect) is both another illustration and an instance of **writing** in general, where the supposed features of writing in the standard sense – as a representational system for transmitting messages in the absence of a sender, such that whatever is sent is structurally liable to be misinterpreted – turn out, on Derrida's argument, to be typical of every signifying act or system of communication. Of course we send letters through the post in the belief that they are destined to reach their intended addressees, just as when we speak to someone we believe our words are destined to be received according to our intentions. We believe that every signifying **event** – every **text** – has an intended destination. But we know from everyday experience that we are sometimes misunderstood when we speak, that we sometimes find ourselves saying something other than what we 'meant' to say, that letters do go missing on occasion, that intentions are always subject to misinterpretation and so on. Or as Eminem puts it wryly, 'I am whatever you say I am / If I wasn't, then why would I say I am?' The point is that our experience of mailing mishaps, or writing effects, is so utterly routine that it's a wonder we ever came to believe in an idea of 'destined' meaning.

Now to be sure every meaning does have to arrive somewhere, just as every letter has to reach a point of arrival – even if we don't happen to know where that is and so we say it got lost or destroyed. But we don't usually think of arrival as containing the possibility of non-arrival, although strictly non-arrival is an end-point and hence a form of arrival (and vice versa). It is for this reason that Derrida coins the term 'adestination' as a way of acknowledging that every letter – every text – has to arrive somewhere, but not necessarily at an intended destination. So every text is destined to arrive, but it is not destined to arrive as intended. Every text, then, is 'adestinal': it is always 'destined' to go to places that exceed the intentions of whoever sends it, regardless of whether the sender is a speaker, an author, a rap artist, a film director, an Internet correspondent or the like.

Derrida uses the example of the postcard to show this 'double' sense of arrival understood in terms of having to include the possibility of non-arrival. Typically, a postcard lends itself to the expression of an almost private language between signatory and addressee (a postcard to a lover, say) or to clichéd descriptions of places and events. As a mode or 'genre' of communication, the postcard is adaptable to the most private and the most public forms of language use. But even in this latter form ('Having a wonderful time. Wish you were here.') the postcard is always intended as a personal message for a particular addressee. Postcards are always intended to be 'private', then, even though they are always open for anyone to read. Such openness compromises not only the privacy of a postcard, but also the general notion of privacy. For no sign or text, no instance of communication whatsoever, could hope to be entirely private or personal, since for anything to signify it has to be constituted already as significatory. For anything to signify, it has to belong to a general system of differential relations that constructs 'it' (a written sign, a facial expression, a cinematic convention) as meaningful. However much a text is intended to be personal (a postcard, a pop song, a novel), its textuality opens it to manifold receptions, readings, interpretations and other unintended and unintentional effects. Nothing can destine a text to mean whatever someone might intend it to mean. Even a private message communicated to a lover is open to the lover's misinterpretation, because everything that is sent – every text – even 'I love you', starts out and can never disentangle itself from the possibility of not arriving as intended, which is to some extent the same as not arriving at all. This condition applies, as should be clear by now, not only to the postal system; it applies to sending, communicating or writing in general, in every possible form (computer-generated texts, everyday speech, works of literature, philosophical treatises, etc.). 'The condition for it to arrive', Derrida writes in reference to the postcard, 'is that it ends up and even that it begins by not arriving' (PC, 29). And this condition is a general condition of texts, of every encounter with a text, whether in the form of reading or writing, sending or receiving. 'This is how it is to be read', as Derrida puts it (ibid.), which could be another way of saying, 'I am whatever you say I am'.

Eminem's refrain seems especially pertinent to Derrida's 'Envois', which takes up the first half of *The Post-Card* and is written in the form of actual postcards sent (by Derrida?) to a lover. It is not possible to say whether the postcards actually ever were sent through the post, but it is precisely this impossibility (or **undecidability**) that deconstructs an ideal of the postcard as a private or personal mode of correspondence. As the sign of a personal relationship between a signatory and an addressee, every post-card (but especially one between lovers) affirms the closeness of the correspondents and at the same time marks their separation. If the signatory and addressee were not apart from one another, there would be no need to send a postcard. But even when they are together, lovers have to express their closeness; they have to send personal messages to each other through their smiles, words, intonations, affectionate touches and the like. Closeness is always something that has to be expressed, that has to be *sent*. In sending closeness, as it were, there is always the risk it will be misunderstood. In being sent, an intended expression of closeness is open to the possibility of not arriving. Even the most intimate expression of love is subject to mailing mishaps – even love is postal. In other words (and who hasn't experienced this?), it is entirely possible to lie to someone that you love them (and of course it's possible also to 'lie' to yourself that you are in love). The point is that the most authentic love in the world can be imitated, which is precisely the principle that makes it impossible to say whether the postcards in 'Envois' are originals or copies, actual or virtual, historical or fictional texts. Generically, they signify authenticity – and there is no way of getting outside that signification, or that form, to something like the real truth of the matter.

Whatever in this case might count as the truth cannot be separated from the text of the matter. The larger point is that this is a general condition, applying just as stubbornly to philosophical texts as to postcards. So one of the effects of 'Envois' (no doubt an intended effect, though that is by the by) is to unsettle the philosophical distinction between the interiority of truth and the exteriority of text. The **logocentric** belief in universal or 'uncontextual' truth (a belief that defines philosophy while also belonging to thought or **metaphysics** in general) denies the irreducible specificity of everything that counts as truth, under particular conditions and circumstances. Here again the postcard is both illustrative and demonstrative. Every postcard is occasional; it is written in a certain place at a certain time by a certain someone who intends to say something personal to a certain someone else. Yet for all that postcards belong undeniably to specific contexts, it must be possible for every postcard to arrive 'out' of context (or not to arrive). In order to reach the intended addressee, it must be possible for a postcard to reach unintended others; in order to be read as intended, it must be possible for it to be read both unintentionally and in unintended ways. While every postcard seems to constitute a 'closed circuit' of exchange between this signatory and that addressee, every postcard is always open – both literally and figuratively, as it were. To intend is to destine, to direct a message from 'me' to 'you'. But in being sent, every message – every text – has to pass through the adestinal provinces and circuits of the postal system. This is not simply a metaphor, which is why Derrida can speak of truth having to pass through 'so many literal pathways, so many correspondences, so many relays' and the like (PC, 94). Every truth, like every letter that we post, is open to the possibility of being misconstrued, taken out of context, received by someone for whom it was not intended. This is precisely because every truth is always in some respects occasional; it comes into being at a certain time, in a certain place, under certain circumstances and conditions. It always holds true, moreover, under certain circumstances and conditions, or within particular contexts, which are always subject to change. Every truth – every text – is always marked by its own singular 'occasionality', but it is always also divided by the fact that no occasion or context is fully determining. This is to acknowledge that all correspondence – personal, philosophical, aesthetic, cinematic, computerized – is occasional; it is always produced with an occasion in mind, in response to contextual needs and expectations, while also being always able to exceed the limits of any particular occasion. In its conditional occasionality, all corres-pondence is always in a sense personal, albeit never exclusively or irreducibly so. But some forms of correspondence – the correspondence of philosophical truths, for example – seek to suppress this condition, on the metaphysical presumption that it is possible to say or mean something outside of a context. What might be called the lesson of 'Envois', then, is not that truth is relative, and certainly not that philosophy is a sham, but rather that truth is contextual and therefore always open to postal effects of misattribution, misdirection, mistiming and so forth. This is not to say that we should give up doing philosophy, or that we should regard philosophical texts as nothing more than occasional pieces with no more authority concerning questions of truth than the postcards we send to our friends when we're on holiday. The lesson of 'Envois' is not that 'Having a wonderful time' is just as philosophical a statement as 'I think, therefore I am'. Rather the lesson is that no text is irreducibly and unalterably philosophical, or not philosophical. Under certain conditions, 'Having a wonderful time' *could* constitute a philosophical statement – and to concede this point is to acknowledge that the question of what philosophy 'is' must involve thinking beyond the opposition of philosophy and text (centre and margin, argument and rhetoric, form and content, truth and representation, etc.) It is to acknowledge that no instance of correspond-ence, or writing, can escape adestination or get outside the post. (See also DIFFERANCE, DISSEMINATION, EVENT, ITERABILITY, PHONOCENTRISM, SUPPLEMENTARITY.)

**presence**   I was asked recently to provide a copy of my signature to one of the administrative sections at the university where I teach, so that by means of digital reproduction it could be made to appear at the bottom of 'personal' letters that were about to be dispatched to prospective students. Every one of those letters will have been signed by me, even though my presence was not required at the time of signing. This tells us something about the structure of the signature – if it were not for **iterability**, no signature could have a unique value. 'In order to function, that is, to be readable, a signature must have a repeatable, iterable, imitable form; it must be able to be detached from the present and singular intention of its production' (LI, 20). But there is also a general lesson here, concerning the **metaphysics** of presence.

It could be said that a digital reproduction of my signature marks the fact of my having once been present in the past, when my 'original' signature was produced. According to this objection, presence would be restored as a necessary condition of every signature in particular and, let's say, of textual production in general. What would be restored would be a sense that every **text**, utterance, correspondence, signifying act or communicative expression (call it what you will) derives from a ground or centre that guarantees it a necessary, essential, undivided and undeconstructible **identity**. So for example the character Gomez in the 1960s TV show *The Addams Family* could be seen as divided from the actor (John Astin) who plays him, but it would seem essential that Ozzy's part in *The Osbournes* is played by Ozzy 'himself'. This would not have the effect of separating living presence from performative or fictional reproduction, since it is possible to maintain that, regardless of who plays the part, the identity of Gomez's character remains undivided. That identity, in other words, is *present* in the 'character', whether of Gomez Addams or Ozzy Osbourne. Even when construed as former, every identity continues to exude a presence that is always there, the undeconstructible **origin** and essence of the identity of every single thing. To play the part of Gomez (whether it be John Astin in the TV series or Raul Julia in the films), an actor must 'return' to the 'essence' of the character 'itself', which is taken always to be present and intact, 'in order *then* to think', as Derrida writes of a general metaphysical succession, 'in terms of derivation, complication, deterioration, accident, etc.' (LI, 93). Since John Astin played the role originally, 'his' Gomez remains present in Raul Julia's performance of the role, even though both actors play the 'same' character whose identity is always present in the character 'itself'. While differences of interpretation are allowable, every actor who plays the part of Gomez would be understood to play the *same* part. It would not seem possible, for instance, to play Gomez *as* Morticia (even though it might be said that Ozzy Osbourne plays a role somewhere between Cousin Itt and Uncle Fester, albeit that is perhaps another matter). Similarly, Charles Addams's originating conception of Gomez's character for the comic strip that became the basis for the TV show, and thereafter the films, remains present in any understanding of what the identity of that character is taken to mean.

This all sounds fine, but it doesn't hold up to much scrutiny. It is not that we could be accused of drawing a long bow in claiming that a cartoon character's identity remains somehow present or 'embodied' in an actor's performance of that character. The problem pertains to a general order of succession, which requires the idea of an undisputed and undeconstructible first or original instance. 'All metaphysicians', Derrida writes, 'from **Plato** to Rousseau, Descartes to Husserl, have proceeded in this way, conceiving good to be before evil, the positive before the negative, the pure before the impure, the simple before the complex, the essential before the accidental, the imitated before the imitation, etc. And this is not just *one* metaphysical gesture among others' (LI, 93). Indeed it's the originating gesture (as it were), '*the* metaphysical exigency, that which has been the most constant, most profound and most potent' (ibid.). Every succession, that is to say, depends on the idea of something coming first, the identity of which is independent of whatever might come after it. So for example 'good' is originary and 'evil' (defined as the absence of good) is secondary, its identity conceived of in terms only of a lapse or fall. But no succession is ever simply linear; it is always also hierarchical. Good both comes before evil and is privileged over it (**speech** comes before and is privileged over **writing**, etc.). In every case, what is considered to be secondary (on both axes) is defined in terms of *the lack of presence*. But try defining good without any recourse whatsoever to a notion of evil. What is 'good' in itself, on its own, in its own right, by virtue of its very nature alone, regarding the essence of itself? How could good ever be *present* to itself, in the absence of evil?

This is to acknowledge that the 'interior presence' of good turns out to depend on a relationship with the 'exterior absence' of evil. Without that relationship, good could never be imputed to exude a presence. (Hence presence is in some sense secondary; it depends on a **structure** of **supplementarity**.) This of course holds true not only for a concept of good, but for every positive or originary concept, text, identity, essence and so forth. Yet still the idea of presence in itself (the self-presence of a thing) persists, and there is no suggestion here that shifting it could ever be a simple matter. 'The history of metaphysics', Derrida writes, 'is the determination of Being as *presence* in all senses of this word. It could be shown that all the names related to fundamentals, to principles, or to the center have always designated an invariable presence' (WD, 279). And how could we ever exchange concepts, for example, if it were not agreed that every concept has an organizing principle, a fundamental essence, a central meaning or identity? How could we even think if we did not believe that thought is present to itself, and present to us, in our thinking? How could we have a concept of the self without believing that, when we think, we are present to ourselves?

Presence – whether we call it 'essence, existence, substance, subject . . . transcendentality, consciousness, God, man, and so forth' (WD, 280) – is 'central' to metaphysics, such that metaphysics is always the metaphysics of presence. This is why Derrida is able to write, in *Of Grammatology*, that making 'enigmatic what one thinks one understands by the words "proximity," "immediacy," "presence" . . . is my final intention in this book' (OG, 70) and, we might add, the final intention of whatever might be understood as the project of **deconstruction** 'itself'. For deconstruction is always a deconstruction of the metaphysics of presence, though always in particular forms.

So resilient and seemingly undeconstructible is the idea of presence that it turns out to persist even, for example, in **Saussure**'s radical concept of the arbitrary structure of the sign. For all that the relationship of signifier to signified is understood as non-transcendental, nevertheless the structure of that relationship itself is always taken to be given and therefore undeconstructible, forming what Derrida calls 'an undecomposable unity' in the privileged relationship of 'the signified and the voice' (OG, 20). 'There has to be a transcendental signified', in other words, 'for the difference between signifier and signified to be somewhere absolute and irreducible' (ibid.). Hence it turns out (contrary to Saussure's own thesis of the arbitrariness of the sign) that the signified is constituted in terms of presence; the signifier in terms of representation. 'The formal essence of the signified is *presence*, and the privilege of its proximity to the logos as *phonè* is the privilege of presence' (OG, 18). If, however, the very idea of 'the transcendental signified' were to be seen simply as another sign (another signifier, an effect of **differance**, the **trace**, **writing** and so on), this might lead to 'the destruction of onto-theology and the metaphysics of presence' (OG, 50). It could be said then that we encounter the necessity of presence to metaphysics in every conception of a totality (the totality of a book, an epoch, class structure, sexual difference, etc.), since every totality is always constituted as the totality of 'the signified [that] preexists it' (OG, 50), remaining present in and to it, and which pre-exists the totality of any sign. (See also BEING, HEIDEGGER, LOGOCENTRISM, PHONOCENTRISM, PROPER, SPECTRALITY.)

**proper**    The word proper (from the Latin *proprius*) has the meaning of 'one's own'. The classical instance of propriety is of course the proper name, which is thought to belong to individuals as one of the very **marks** of individuality. I don't answer to just any name – I answer to 'my' name only. In this way my proper name seems to be essential to my sense of **identity**, despite the fact that my proper name is not strictly my exclusive property. My 'proper' name, in other words, has been given to me from within a system of coded possibilities. If my name were truly proper, if it were truly mine exclusively, no one – including myself – would know how to say it, to repeat it, to exchange it. No one could even know it *as* a name. Even if someone had a name that had never been used before in history (remember when Prince changed his name to a symbol, which no one could *say* at all?), it could function as a name only to the extent that it could be recognized as conforming to a code. Every proper name, then, is made up of common signifying elements, which do not belong to anyone. So the propriety of 'one's own' proper name relies on being formed out of general signifying elements that are *not* one's own – elements that are im-proper. Impropriety is every proper name's condition of possibility. 'The expression "proper name"', as Derrida puts it, 'is improper', because what the expression seeks to mark – the absolute individuality of the individual – is impossible (OG, 111). Every proper name is 'a linguistico-social classi-fication' (ibid.); it belongs to impropriety before and in order to become 'one's own'.

What is it that we could call 'one's own' if not the unique self-**presence** of individual **being**? But this is precisely what is not contained within a proper name, which in order to be a name has to be comprised of elements belonging to a general system of naming or classification. Every proper name gestures to an absolute individuality that it cannot name except in general (improper) terms. In a sense, every proper name names a certain 'loss of the proper, of absolute proximity, of self-presence' (OG, 112). A proper name marks the unique individuality of the individual only from within a general system of 'linguistico-social classification'; from the beginning the individual proper is lost within that system. But what is 'the individual' outside a system of social relations? The lost presence of the individual, in other words, is a 'loss' that never happened; it is 'the loss of what has never taken place, of a self-presence which has never been given but only dreamed of and always already split, repeated, incapable of appearing to itself except in its own disappearance' (ibid.).

This should not be taken to imply that Derrida or **deconstruction** is unconcerned with individuals. The point rather is that individuality depends on an 'experience of the impossible' (SoM, 65), because individuality is never 'one's own' – nothing that is individual is ever at one with 'itself'. There is no individual proper outside 'its' relations to others, such that every individual person or thing is always already divided from within. Individuality begins not in presence but in difference. In order to do **justice** to individuals, then, it is necessary to acknowledge what is im-proper and im-possible about individuals, including 'one's own' individuality. This entails a **responsibility** ('an ethical and political duty') to account for what Derrida calls the 'impossibility of being one with oneself' (VR , 14). It is this impossibility – or this impropriety – that is the basis of our relations with others. 'It is because I am not one with myself', as Derrida puts it, 'that I can speak with the other and address the other' (ibid.). If we were to conceive of the individual in terms only of propriety, then, we would in fact deny the absolute and radical individuality (or singularity) of every individual as such. It is to the extent only that individuals are allowed not to have to conform to notions of propriety – allowed not to have to go through the proper channels in order to make proper demands on us, or not to have to conduct themselves according to a proper mode of being – that individuals have any individuality at all. (See also DEMOCRACRY, DIFFERANCE, EVENT, GIFT, ITERABILITY, META-PHYSICS, ORIGIN, SPECTRALITY, TRACE.)

**responsibility**   During a press interview while on tour with The Rolling Stones in Australia in February 2003, Keith Richards scandalized local authorities by declaring that drugs are not a problem in themselves: the problems associated with drug use are social. It isn't drugs that fuck you up, but the debilitating lifestyle of the drug user (a socially enforced routine of crime and desperation) that does all the damage. Now of course this view was roundly condemned in the media by medical practitioners, politicians, church leaders, social workers and the like, who were outraged that Richards had abused his responsibility as a 'role model' to the young (he's 59 years old!) by not sending a clear message that drugs are unconditionally dangerous.

But the question here is not about the pros and cons of drug taking; it's about the nature of responsibility. We all know what is meant when a celebrity is accused of 'failing' as a role model: it means that he or she is seen as 'irresponsible' for not having used a position of supposed influence to endorse a standard notion of morality or good citizenship. But what if someone like Keith Richards, say, is in fact a role model – it's just that he's a role model for unorthodox, nonconformist, anti-authoritarian, self-questioning individualism? (Never mind that we may not be convinced by such a model or that 'nonconformity' might be a privilege that Richards can exercise because of his personal wealth. It is not the self-**presence** of psychological or economic subjectivity but rather the interpretability of **text** that occupies us here.) Wouldn't he have a responsibility, in that case, to speak out against the idea that **proper** social **being** is defined in accordance with standards that have been sanctioned by the state, the church, the legal system, health professionals and so on? Paradoxically, then, in order to be responsible to an anti-authoritarian sense of the proper, he would have to risk appearing irresponsible to those for whom 'being responsible' amounts to following a predetermined course or programme of socially acceptable things to say and do.

This is not to suggest that responsibility should be defined as whatever happens to be said and done for the sake (or even in the name) of being anti-authoritarian or oppositional. Responsibility is irreducible either to a programme (a code of ethics, a set of social obligations or political duties) or the opposite of a programme (intuition, solipsism, anarchy). What Derrida calls responsibility's 'condition of possibility' consists of an **aporia**: it has to do with the impossible possibility of a prescribed or general 'choice' that is also a 'personal' or singular decision. 'I will even venture to say', he writes, 'that ethics, politics, and responsibility, *if there are any*, will only ever have begun with the experience and experiment of the aporia' (OH, 41). For if, in order to be responsible, all we need to do is to follow a prescribed course of action or a general plan, then we would never have to make a decision to be responsible. This would be the very measure of irresponsibility. But if we never had to take any account at all of social, ethical, political or other pressures to be responsible according to the rules of a system, any 'decision' to be responsible would be of the order of a self-gratifying whim or a romantic self-validation. This too would belong to irresponsibility. So what Derrida means by responsibility (I leave aside the question of what Keith Richards might mean by this) involves having to come to terms with the **undecidability** of differences between and within prescribed and personal decisions. A fully prescribed decision would not be a decision, since no responsibility would be involved in making it. A fully personal decision would not be a decision either, since you wouldn't have to be accountable for making it beyond saying that it 'felt right' for you. Neither responsibility by numbers, then, nor by intuition. 'The condition of possibility of this thing called responsibility', as Derrida puts it, 'is a certain *experience and experiment of the possibility of the impossible*' (OH, 41). As he writes elsewhere, 'without this experience of the impossible, one might as well give up on both **justice** and the **event**' (SoM, 65). We could never acknowledge the socially wretched 'event-ness' of the drug user's existence, for example, unless the concept of event were allowed to mean something more than what happens simply by personal choice. A decision to go to war, or to adopt a certain lifestyle, isn't reducible to an expression of individual or collective 'will'. So a decision to see the condemned or disadvantaged existence of drug users as a social, political or economic *event* involves having to take responsibility for others, and of course also for ourselves. And it may involve having to see the event-ness of what Derrida describes as 'the growing and undelimitable, that is, world-wide power of those super-efficient and properly capitalist phantom-States that are the mafia and the drug cartels on every continent' (SoM, 83). The responsibility for the problems of drug usage, in other words, cannot be confined to the 'personal' choices of drug users. As social beings we have to take responsibility for everything that happens socially, which is an inexhaustible and overwhelming task. And what happens socially cannot be allowed to be reduced to what happens according to a concept of event as **presence** or to an idea of justice as determined by the law. This is why Derrida argues that 'there is no responsibility without a dissident and inventive rupture with respect to tradition, authority, orthodoxy, rule, or doctrine' (GoD, 27). We could never say that democratic doctrine demands that we invade Iraq, for instance, or that in order to defend Western tradition we are obliged to oppose Palestinian claims to sovereignty. But neither could we say that the concept of **democracy** is free of all things doctrinaire, having nothing whatsoever to do with authority and rule. So in order to make responsible decisions – in response to democracy, to justice, to the otherness of others – we can't just make it up as we go along, and we can't defer to the steadfast authority of a pre-existing doctrine or programme.

Nor can we hope that our decisions will be guided by some pre-existing force or 'spirit', as the **Heidegger** of 'The Rectorship Address' (1933) argued on behalf of the German university. In his inaugural speech at Freiburg, Heidegger maintained that all members of the 'German' university community (teachers, administrators and students alike, albeit the category 'university administrator' is perhaps anachronistic here) owed 'their existence and their strength only to a true common rootedness in the essence of the German university' (cited in OS, 34). This essence could reveal itself, however, only when the teachers (the ones who guide, the *Führer*) themselves submitted to spiritual supervision, giving in to being 'guided by the inflexibility of this spiritual mission [*jenes geistige Auftrags*], the constraining nature of which imprints the destiny of the German people with its specific historical character' (ibid.). The point here is not to expose Heidegger's complicity with Nazism (which is not, in any case, a straightforward matter) but rather to show that if the decisions of the Third Reich found their justification in a notion of universal spirit or cultural destiny, to which even a philosopher as eminent as Heidegger may have resorted, there is nothing especially remarkable about this. History is full of ineffable, transcendental 'things' – democracy, freedom, progress, the Enlightenment, Western tradition, human nature – to which we are supposed to be responsible and which are supposed to guide us in making responsible (or 'tough') decisions. But Derrida's radical sense of responsibility is always set adrift from a pre-existing, pre-formed, a priori *anything*, which is why (for Derrida) you could never let yourself think – in a moment of 'clock time', as it were – that you *are* responsible. Even Heidegger's attempt to locate a 'non-metaphysical' *spirit* as the justification for a responsibility to be critical or questioning – to be (in a sense) 'deconstructive' – turns out to rely on a familiar **metaphysics** in its dependence on that spirit as a guiding force, however much that force or spirit 'itself' is inexplicable (according to Heidegger) from within metaphysics (see OS, 51–66). As soon as responsibility is cut loose even from something as elusive as 'spirit' as a ground of justification, nothing could be said to justify a decision – nothing could be said to ground a decision as just or responsible. At such a moment (which would always be outside time as measured by a clock) there could never be an end to responsibility: responsibility would always remain to be done. In response to this you could say only that one is always 'never responsible enough' (GoD, 51). (See also DIFFERANCE, GIFT, HYMEN, *KHORA*, MESSIANISM, NEW INTERNATIONAL, SPECTRALITY, YES.)

**Saussure, Ferdinand de** (Swiss linguist, 1857–1913)  The founder of European semiotics (or semiology), Saussure is responsible for the radical concept of the 'arbitrary' **structure** of the sign. This structure depends on a distinction between what he calls the *signifier* (or sound-image) and the *signified* (or mental concept), both of which are indispensable to the constitution of any sign as a signifying unit. The relationship between any signified (think of a cat) and a signifier (the word 'cat'), however, is arbitrary, by which Saussure means simply that the relationship isn't natural or necessary. There is no determined reason, that is to say, why 'cat' should make us think of a cat, otherwise you would expect that a cat would be called a 'cat' in every language – and according to this logic there ought to be only one language in the world. The fact that there are many languages, and that languages evolve, is because of the arbitrary or undetermined structure of the sign. What 'cat' means in English, then, doesn't have anything to do with cats as such, but rather with the differences between 'cat' and other English words. We recognize that 'cat' refers to a cat because 'cat' is not 'dog', for instance, but also (more specifically) because it isn't 'sat', 'fat' or 'bat' and so on. From this we can say that all signs signify by virtue of their relations to general differences ('cat' isn't 'dog', or 'philosophy') and specific differences or structural similarities ('cat' isn't 'bat'). In the case of words, although the principle applies to signs of every kind, we can think of these structural similarities as effects of rules. So if you were asked to make an English word of three letters using the suffix '-at', you would know that you'd be precluded by the rules of the language from choosing to combine '-at' with the letters 'a' or 'i'. Now, for Saussure, such rules belong to what he calls the *langue* of any language (or any system of signs), or we could think of *langue* as a set of conditions of possibility for signs generally. These rules or conditions cannot be accessed directly; they can only ever be *inferred*, on the basis of signs in actual use. Saussure calls the use of any sign, or any actual instance of sign usage, an example of *parole*.

Derrida's problem with all this is that, despite its radical import, Saussure's theory of meaning cannot get away from **presence** as a ground of differences. It must be stressed that **deconstruction** would be impossible within the limits of a pre-Saussurean concept of the sign, but nevertheless the difference between Saussure's signifier and signified, as with the difference between *langue* and *parole*, is grounded in a **metaphysics** of presence. The question of where differences comes from, in a word, is never quite asked by Saussure, which is why (as Derrida argues at length in the *Grammatology*) he cannot quite think past, or never quite disturbs, a standard form of the **speech–writing opposition**. (See also APORIA, DIFFERANCE, LOGOCENTRISM, PHONOCENTRISM, SUPPLEMENTARITY, WRITING.)

**self-presence**  See **presence**.

**spectrality**  You don't have to believe in ghosts to be affected by them. The ghost is a powerful figure, regardless of whether or not you credit it with some kind of actual existence. Indeed it could be said that the ghost's very power itself comes precisely from not being able to choose between 'whether or not' – whether or not it is, for example. In its **undecidability**, then, the ghost's ontology cannot be of the order of the difference between life and death, say, or the actual and the virtual. We might not believe in ghosts, but can we say that ghosts are therefore absolutely unreal, not belonging in any sense at all to what we call reality? If so, then surely we would have to reconsider our faith in an idea of the future, if not our faith in *possibility* as such, or simply even our *faith* in all its possible forms. Because like the ghost, if we do not believe in it and think it isn't real since it has no existence, the future is without existence too, albeit we believe that one day it will come to exist.

No one would say the future isn't real. No one would say that the past, although it no longer exists, isn't real either. So our sense of reality includes things that we might otherwise associate with the unreal, and we neither see nor experience any contradiction in this. My dead parents, my dead marriage, my dead friends – these are all real and unreal at the same time, which is to say that they are very real indeed even though they don't exist any more. The generations to come are real as well, even though they don't exist yet.

What seems to be at stake here is what is meant by existence. The dead and the generations to come don't, in a sense, exist, but in some other sense they do. They exist in the same way as the ghost exists, beyond the opposition of existence and non-existence, life and death, actuality and virtuality and so on. This is why (in *Specters of Marx*) Derrida takes to writing about ghosts, because the ghost puts into question what it means to exist, what it means to be – or not to be. So for all that it's a book about Marx and, as it were, about politics; for all that it is, in a sense, Derrida's most overtly 'political' book (even, in a way, his most important one), *Specters of Marx* is also another entrée into the question of **presence**. For what kind of thing is the ghost or the spectre but that which confounds the question of what and where it is? As Derrida puts it, 'what is the *being-there* of a specter? what is the mode of presence of a specter? that is the only question we would like to pose here' (SoM, 38).

It is well known that this question confronts and confounds Shakespeare's Hamlet, and so it is unsurprising that *Hamlet* should turn out to be the inspiration for an understanding of spectrality. In the appearance, which is also the re-appearance, of 'the thing' at the beginning of the play, all that **metaphysics** allows or constrains us to regard as certain (concerning time, **identity**, presence and so forth) is opened to the risk of becoming uncertain, of coming undone or being disjoined. The decision to give the thing a name – it 'is' (the spectre of) the dead King – cannot close off that risk. Once the question of how to decide the difference between certainty and uncertainty is opened, there can be no possibility of returning to a past when every *thing* had its place on one side or the other of the opposition between life and death, real and unreal, **being** and phantasm. For **deconstruction**, of course, there never was such a past; there has never been a time without ghosts. The opening within metaphysics has always been there from the start, whenever that might have been and whatever might be the mode of presence or the being-there of an opening. What is the presence of a gap, an absence?

So whatever the spectral effects of the ghost in *Hamlet*, they cannot be confined to that play or consigned to products of the imagination or the work of literature in general. Spectrality is not (or not only) a literary or fictive 'thing', something we allow 'to be' within the space of a certain kind of writing that we let 'play around' with notions of reality, being and the like. The being-there of the ghost is irreducible to an aesthetic zone or an order of thinking delimited by 'poetic licence'. Yet for metaphysics, it is precisely within the **textual** field and specificity (whatever that might be) of literature that 'the virtual space of spectrality' (SoM, 11) is located. Literature is allowed to play games with reality, to speculate about things we know (for certain) could never exist or happen. Against this excessive space of the literary, the real world of real things and real **events** is all the better defined. This is not simply a distinction held by scientists, political pragmatists or people with common sense. The distinction is dear to metaphysics in general and runs all the way through specialist or scholarly thinking in particular. Scholars don't believe in ghosts. 'There has never been a scholar who, as such, does not believe in the sharp distinction between the real and the unreal, the actual and the inactual, the living and the non-living, being and non-being' (SoM, 11). Spectrality, then, as a name or a 'nickname' (something other than a **proper** name) for the *non-opposition* of the real and the unreal, being and non-being, etc., has to be engaged and thought from somewhere outside the difference between scholarly thought and its others (pure fancy, wishful thinking, intuition, ingenious speculation and so on). This takes courage – the courage, perhaps, to risk going mad.

Hamlet for one certainly takes that risk; and whether or not he goes mad for a while, or feigns a temporary madness for strategic effect, is not the point. In having to think about spectrality, Hamlet has to think differently; he has to think *difference* differently, as it were. (And this is a far cry from standard accounts of his 'procrastination'.) Once there is the ghost, the very question of what 'there is' *means* becomes undecidable. At the same time, the ghost's presence (whatever it might be) calls up the question of what to do about it, and of what to do about what the incorporeal spectre says about the body politic of Denmark and what must be done about that. In a sense, the more Hamlet faces up to 'the virtual space of spectrality', or the more he tries to think difference differently, the more he becomes aware of his obligation to make a political decision, a decision that has to be made out of respect for his father's memory, the authority of his own position as heir to the role of sovereign-protector, the political interests of his subjects and, of course and perhaps above all, out of respect simply for **justice**. It could be that in thinking so much, if not also so courageously, Hamlet is being philosophical (it's no accident that *Hamlet* is sometimes called Shakespeare's most philosophical play), but he is never not always being political at the same time.

Yet what 'political' might mean in this context is closer to something like an encounter with the im-possible than to a standard sense of politics referring to a programme or position marked out in advance. Hamlet is never political in the standard sense. The political reckoning of his actions, and inactions, proceeds not from a direct or conscious choice to oppose power, but from the fact that while he never quite recoils from a sense of **responsibility**, he knows that, in itself, responsibility is unprogrammable and inexhaustible. In this way responsibility entails the impossibility of knowing that it must be done *and* knowing that it can never be done, since it is not possible to fulfil one's responsibility (or responsibilities) in the strictest sense – responsibility always remains to be done (or 'to come'). One effect of the ghost in Shakespeare's play is to foreground the sense in which responsibility is overwhelming: the ghost is there (but where?) to remind Hamlet of his duty – to his living subjects, to be sure, but also to his dead father and more generally to ideals of sovereignty and justice. This is what disjoins or unhinges time ('The time is out of joint', as Hamlet says), such that the alignment of the dead with the living constitutes a kind of impossible temporality. Like the ghost, this alignment cannot be located within historical time. But the spectral time, or the spectrality, of this alignment is also perfectly mundane. Everyone knows that responsibility extends not only to the living but also to the dead and those who are yet to be born. So we might say that what ghosts do (regardless of any belief in them) is to intensify something we already know. Yet we might also say that, like Hamlet, we are prone to forgetful-ness and need ghosts to remind us of our responsibility, if not to remind us that responsibility is always overwhelming.

This might seem a long way from politics. On Derrida's account, though, the question of spectrality is central to an understanding of Marx and therefore, let's say, to any politics that would want to be responsible to an ideal of justice or a just society. Marx was the first to conceive of an international labour movement organized against established systems of control. The **'new' international** would oppose 'old' power; **democracy** would overcome privilege. This was Marx's promise. Without denying Marx's deep sense of history, it cannot be denied either that the communist project was and remains spectral in its effects. The question here concerns alignment. As a promise, communism (which is aligned to an ideal of democracy) remains to come. What, then, is its time? And what is an international alignment except one without limit. What, then, is its place? The question doesn't go away simply because there *were* communist governments in the world at certain times, or because some countries still *are* communist (without being democratic) today. Marx's promise can't be said not to have been kept just because communism has failed, in historical time, to live up to it, or because neo-liberalism triumphed over communism when the Soviet Union 'collapsed'. These positions could be held only in a world without ghosts. First of all, to suppose that communism, like Marx, is dead, that its time is over, would be to deny something like the revolutionary spirit or promise within communism (or Marxism) which can't be separated from it. And this would be to suppose, secondly, that today's present time supersedes a past present when time was out of joint because of communism's ever-present threat to global stability or world order, which of course as everyone knows depends on the unhindered operations of the 'free market'. In the past, then, when there was communism, the future was put at risk. The today of the past was lived under the threat of global nuclear war, which meant that there might be no tomorrow. So when communism was defeated, the future was (re)assured. But how can the future be guaranteed 'without *concluding in advance*, without reducing in advance both the future and its chance? Without totalizing in advance?' (SoM, 37). To see the future is to see what always remains invisible, inactual, non-present and spooky in its insubstantiality. To suppose to know what the future will look like requires absolute faith in the opposition of life and death, being and non-being, actuality and ineffectivity and so forth; it requires being certain that there is no such thing as a ghost, which is the same as being certain of what every thing actually *is*. Such totalizing faith is one thing, but what things actually are is quite another.

Nevertheless, faith of any kind is always less than actual or objective and to some extent therefore always spectral in nature. Even faith in the difference between the actual and the inactual is less than actual itself. So if the figure of the ghost helps us to see not the difference but the **differance** between 'objective' reality and figural 'reality', it should also help us to see that pronouncements on the death of communism, Marxism, Marx and the left are premature, no more perhaps than expressions of wishful thinking on the part of Marx's adversaries and of a loss of faith among his advocates. For no one can predict the future. After all, the world today includes *Sir* Mick Jagger! Who would ever have thought the future could come to look like that? Without having to anticipate that one day even Eminem might be welcomed into the establishment, it remains the case that there is nothing certain about the future. All the same, according to a certain habit of thought (common to both sides of politics and to every nation state) the future has to be planned for, on the basis not of what it could but what it *should* become, as if it were merely a continuation of the present or a projection of the present beyond 'itself'. For every politics, we might say, the future must be programmed. This is true for Marx himself, and for Marxist politics. But it needs to be seen that the promise of an international alliance, an alliance beyond the control of any nation and outside the borders of every nation, against power and privilege, against the 'free' market, against the 'free' flow of capital, information and ideas, takes us to the limit not just of political practicality but of thought. This is not to undermine but rather to affirm the liberatory force of that promise. 'Not only', as Derrida writes, 'must one not renounce the emancipatory desire [of Marx's promise], it is necessary to insist on it more than ever, it seems, and insist on it, moreover, as the very indestructibility of the "it is necessary." This is the condition of a re-politicization, perhaps of another concept of the political' (SoM, 75).

It would lessen the force of that 'emancipatory desire' if Marx's promise, or the promise of Marxism (one that might remain to come), were to be conceived of today, in the present, in terms only of what we are able to imagine might become actual in the future, based on our experience and knowledge of the past. What the future holds is undecidable, but this doesn't mean that the present and the past are wholly calculable, objective, actual, real and the like in contrast to the future's phantasmagoric non-presence. That opposition came undone at the first sign of a ghost. Nor does the spectrality of Marx's promise turn it into an airy-fairy wish for things to get better, or mean that because of its 'impracticality' the promise was never anything more than a romantic, idealist or ideological dream. An emancipatory desire for (as it were) unrealizable emancipation, for emancipation without limit (beyond geographical and historical borders), is all the more necessary, Derrida insists, now that Marxism can be spoken of as having run its course, run out of ideas, imploded. There are many dangers, for both sides of politics, in pronouncing Marxism dead, in thinking that the 'spectre' of communism has been expelled. For what other political project has ever been driven by an impossible emancipatory desire – not simply a desire for self-determination on the part of a certain group or people, but a desire for emancipation on a scale exceeding imagination? If Marxism is dead, if that desire no longer has any organizing force, what hope the future? When, for example, conservatives speak of emancipation, they mean the freedom of capital to go wherever it likes, unrestricted by national laws and borders, union regulations, land rights and so on, or the freedom of employers to go on being economically productive, unrestrained by wage demands, claims for improved working conditions, health and safety issues and the like. They don't mean emancipation on a scale exceeding imagination, for the whole world. Capitalist emancipation and spectral (or 'communist') emancipation are different, to be sure, and there is no question that deconstruction is on the side of the ghostly when it comes to desiring freedom.

But this is not quite to say that deconstruction is on the side of Marxism, though it's certainly not opposed to it: 'deconstruction would have been impossible and unthinkable in a pre-Marxist space', Derrida writes (SoM, 92). The problem with Marxism, at least in the forms in which it has been actualized or imagined, is that its emancipatory desire isn't quite spectral enough; in any case, the spectrality of that desire has never quite been acknowledged. And this goes back to Marx himself, who was no great lover of ghosts, even though, in a sense, ghosts were just about all he ever thought of (the spectres of communist revolution, organized labour, radical equality, for example). To respond to Marx's promise today, then, requires an adherence to or faith in a certain idea of Marxism and at the same time requires that that faith be broken or disavowed, all the better to respond responsibly to the promise. This is to say that any Marxism that would try to programme the future (which is every Marxism and Marxist, including Marx himself, until now) would always be less than true to an ideal of Marxism, would always break faith with the revolutionary emancipatory desire that distinguishes Marxism from all other politics. The future is unprogrammable; the emancipatory desire that exceeds imagination must include the desire to emancipate the present from ideas of a programmed future.

This notion of a radically unforeseeable future which remains forever open and to come is precisely what every politics, every political programme, turns a blind eye to. But in turning away from spectrality, in avoiding the question of the being-there of the ghost, every politics is less responsible than it should be to an emancipatory desire for a better world. To avoid the being-there of the ghost is to avoid being true to justice. While justice never simply happens on its own, neither can it be programmed for. In this way justice, like the future, necessitates an 'experience of the impossible' (SoM, 65), such as the question of the being-there, the presence, of a spectre. A politics that couldn't ask that question (or which couldn't see it) would presume to know the difference between us and them, and would presume to be able to shape or control the future according to its own interests. It would do so, moreover, on the presumption of a right to determine what is to come, to take charge of the future by controlling it in advance, directing it towards a predetermined end. What should be guiding us instead, according to Derrida, is an experience of the impossible, which is in fact the very 'condition of possibility' of the future – and of justice (SoM, 65). In what is no doubt a 'new' sense of the political (albeit one that still bears a **trace** of Marx's revolutionary promise, or promisory revolution), we might say that in order to be political we must let ourselves be guided by ghosts. (See also ARTIFACTUALITY, GIFT, MESSIANISM, POSTAL METAPHOR, TELETECHNOLOGY, VIRTUALITY, YES.)

**speech–writing opposition**    The fact we all learned to speak before we learned to write mirrors (or seems to mirror) the fact that speech came before **writing** historically. Everyone from **Plato** to **Saussure** and beyond has thought this way about the **origin** and evolution of human communication: speech first, then writing. But for Derrida this way of thinking is true in so far only as the speech–writing 'succession' is understood in terms of the speech–writing *opposition*, which depends on writing being understood only in a literal or in an empirical sense. Defined as a system of literal inscriptions (or graphic representations) writing can be seen to come after speech once it has been allowed that speech comes first not simply as a matter of historical 'fact', but according to its associations with 'nature' and 'truth'. These associations – these values – constitute the historico-**metaphysical** fact of speech's priority to and over writing, and they depend on a concept of **intentionality** as **presence**. Spoken language is 'natural', then, because it emanates from the minds and bodies of living speakers who mean (or intend) what they say and say what they mean without recourse to prosthetic or technological devices. The presence of the speaker guarantees the truth of what is said.

With this understanding of speech in place, writing is doomed to perform a secondary (or representational) role as a technology for copying the truth of spoken language. Writing as 'written-down speech' is condemned to be inferior to speech. But in every account of this 'succession' Derrida notices the necessity of an opposition: in order for spoken words to be attributed the status of 'non-representational' truth, speech has to be opposed to writing as representation. It is this – the speech–writing opposition – which has to be in place before speech can be said to come before writing.

Only when the differential, **supplementary** or **disseminatory** effects of this opposition are ignored is it possible for speech to appear self-sufficient and independent, its origin and history seeming ideally to be unaffected by the operations of writing. Take the example of Saussure. By locating the origin of human communication in the indivisible unity of thought and sound (thought and *spoken* sign) Saussure confines writing to mean only, as Derrida points out, 'a certain type of writing: phonetic writing' (OG, 30). According to this originary unity there is no choice but to think of writing as written-down speech. 'Writing will be "phonetic," it will be the outside, the exterior representation of language and of this "thought-sound." It must necessarily operate from already constituted units of signification, in the formation of which it has played no part' (OG, 31). But, Derrida asks, if these 'already constituted units of significa-tion' (the veritable *inside* of language) are in fact sufficient unto themselves, why does Saussure spend so much time talking about writing? Why does 'he give so much attention to that external phenomenon, that exiled figuration, that outside, that double' (OG, 34)? His apparent reason for doing so is that (like Plato, Rousseau and many others) Saussure is con-cerned to warn against the dangers of writing, such that for him (but not for him alone) writing has what Derrida calls 'the exteriority that one attributes to utensils; to what is even an imperfect tool and a dangerous, almost maleficent, technique' (ibid.). And what's so dangerous about writing? The general answer to this is that writing is associated tradition-ally 'with the fatal violence of the political institution' (the 'fall' into culture, as it were), constituting an originary 'break with nature' (OG, 36). In Saussure's *Course in General Linguistics* this takes the particular form of the substitution of a 'natural' *phonic* **mark** (sound) by an 'artificial' *graphic* mark (image). After there was writing (so the story goes) words came to be associated with their written forms. Hence 'the spoken word is so intimately bound to its written *image*', according to Saussure, 'that the latter manages to *usurp* the main role' (cited in OG, 36).

All the same, what's being protected or preserved here is not, on Derrida's account, the purity of speech as such, but what might be called a certain ideal of the purity of purity. The idea that *there just is* purity, authenticity, originality, **identity**, truth, nature and so on – prior to and independent of any system of writing, outside of any need to express, convey, argue for or otherwise represent the 'self-reliance' of the pure, the authentic, the original, etc. – is what Saussure's argument is protecting, albeit not con-sciously or deviously. In other words it is a metaphysical requirement that speech has to come before writing: Saussure's argument simply conforms to that requirement, and is not alone in doing so.

Because, moreover, this requirement belongs only within metaphysics (and is not true always and everywhere) it has to be produced as if it were always already true, always and everywhere. And the only way to produce it is to talk about writing as the 'outside' of the 'inside', which is to 'produce' it by way of repeating it: the **inside–outside** opposition, then, is but a variation on the speech–writing opposition (and of course vice versa). Without the presumption of an undeconstructible bottom line, there is no metaphysics. So in order to preserve metaphysics (but not consciously or deviously) Saussure has to resort to defining the inside (speech) in terms of features he associates with the outside (writing), whose origin and history he regards as having nothing to do with the formation of 'already constituted units of signification' that are independent of laws pertaining to the **structure** of graphic marks.

Dazzled by the visibility of writing, we are blind to the pre-eminence of speech. Saussure calls this the 'trap' that all linguists have fallen into, the trap of confusing language and writing. 'This explains', Derrida argues, 'why *The Course in General Linguistics* treats *first* this strange external system that is writing. As necessary preamble to restoring the natural to itself, one must first disassemble the trap' (OG, 37). And yet it is precisely here, at the beginning, that the work of restoring speech to full presence ('restoring the natural to itself') comes unstuck. For no matter how much Saussure wants to locate the sign's origin in nature, in the natural language of speech, his every effort to define the essence of the spoken sign keeps on turning out to rely on the written sign as the model of that essence. Writing, the excluded outside of language, keeps on having to be brought back 'into' language in order to define the *identity* of that which does not owe its identity to writing. What is taken to be exterior and 'post', as it were, presents an idea of the interior and the prior. The very idea of something being pre- or non-representational turns out to be an effect of representation. 'The system of language associated with phonetic-alphabetic writing', as Derrida puts it, 'is that within which **logocentric** metaphysics, determining the sense of **being** as presence, has been produced' (OG, 43). Here we can see that Derrida's discussion of the speech–writing opposition is not designed to improve or correct linguistics; its aim rather is to intervene in the determination of being-as-presence (understood as subjectivity or consciousness, for example). In order for that determination to survive, for what Derrida calls 'this *epoch* of the full speech' to continue, it has always been necessary to exclude or suspend 'all free reflection on the origin and status of writing . . . which was not *technology* and the *history of a technique*' (ibid.). The idea that *there just is* purity, authenticity, originality, identity, truth, nature and so on, depends on writing having to be understood only as a technology for copying speech. This narrow conception of writing as written-down speech both preserves and produces such ideas as the before-and-after of representation and the inside-and-outside of presence. Hence it is possible to think of the speech–writing succession (in terms of the historio-metaphysical privileging of speech as the origin of language) on the basis only of the speech–writing opposition; it's possible to think of speech coming before writing only because writing must come before speech.

It ought to be clear at this point that what Derrida means by writing is irreducible to 'phonetic writing' or to writing in the literal or empirical sense. If his 'writing' did mean that, then it would be preposterous to claim that writing comes before speech – as if we all came into the world scrambling about madly for a pen and notepad in order quickly to jot down our name and what we want out of life and thereafter, about six to eight months later, started saying 'da-da' and 'goo-goo'. That is emphatically not what the **deconstruction** of the speech–writing opposition entails. But think about what has to be in place in order to suppose (as many do) that Derrida's attempt at putting writing before speech defies all logic. Doesn't one have to have in mind already an idea of Derrida as a complete idiot – the Elvis of basket cases, the James Brown of the 'super mad', the Tu Pac of all crazies – for having gone on now for over forty years thinking that writing must come before speech without it ever once occurring to him that he himself had had to learn to talk before learning to write?

Derrida has never denied that speech comes before phonetic writing. His point is that phonetic writing (writing as written-down speech) is only a form of a more general writing, or a more general concept of writing, which generates the possibility of speech as *presence*, as *origin* of language, as *natural* communication. This general writing can be glimpsed in Saussure's own thesis of the arbitrariness of the sign, although Saussure himself couldn't see it. For what is the arbitrary sign if not what Derrida calls the 'instituted **trace**' (OG, 46)? Saussure did not mean that the signifier–signified relationship is arbitrary in the sense of being haphazard or random, as though whenever someone uses the sign 'apple' it is entirely a matter of chance as to what others might interpret it to mean. On the contrary, the thesis of the arbitrariness of the sign accounts for the fact that there is no a priori reason why 'apple' should signify a particular kind of edible fruit. That it does signify a particular kind of edible fruit has to do with an historico-institutional agreement. The relationship between 'apple' and 'red, green or yellow fruit, good for eating' had to be instituted; it wasn't just there lying on the ground, or floating up in the ether, waiting to be found. Every signifier–signified relationship has to be instituted (which does not mean only that it has to be institutionalized) – instituted from within an overall system of differences which generates meaning. So the arbitrary relationship of signifier to signified is an instituted relationship, and this goes a long way towards dismantling the idea that signs are produced by the determination of presence. Indeed, as Derrida points out, it goes a long way towards dismantling the very concept of the sign as such. On Saussure's own account, that is, no sign can signify on its own and so every sign is always (as Derrida remarks) 'a sign of a sign' (OG, 43) – every signified, another signifier. In this respect no sign ever quite comes into being or presence; no sign ever quite establishes itself as a unit in its own right but is forever caught up in a **play** or network of differential relations with other signs. There is nothing outside of this play, 'nothing outside of the **text**' (OG, 158). Hence (although Saussure never quite saw it this way) the structure of the signifier–signified relationship refers not so much to the sign as a signifying entity in itself, the sign 'as such', but to something seemingly far less ontological or phenomenological – the *trace*.

A trace is the sign of an absent presence, a sign of a sign. It is an almost indecipherable mark of the imputed fact that something which is not here now was here beforehand, that something which was present – in a seemingly former version of the present here-and-now (a former present) – is gone, never to return. Every trace marks the absence of a presence. At the same time it preserves an ideal of presence as such, as what everything has to have (or to have had), even though it is precisely only the loss or absence of presence that the trace can register. So the structure of the trace is less determinate than the structure of the sign, because the latter still depends on an idea of unity consisting of *this* signifier being drawn (however arbitrarily) along a path leading to *that* rather than to some other or just any signified. To trace is to draw or to make one's way – to leave an impression by hand or foot, as it were. The English word 'trace' carries both these senses, referring to a barely perceptible inscription (an impression of some kind) and also to a path, a trail or a track – a *way*. The spoor, for example, of a wild animal ('spoor' is one of the meanings of the French word *trace*) indicates a tracing of its way through the bush or countryside, but is made up of nothing so substantial as 'already constituted units of signification'; it consists rather of broken twigs, depressions in the grass, marks in the sand. To follow a spoor, or to recognize anything as a trace, involves active interpretation; it means having to make decisions, having to sift, to sort and to speculate. The way of the trace, then, is 'adestinal' or **postal** – it does not describe a destined path from one determined point to another, from this signifier to that signified (for instance). This is the sense in which the thesis of the arbitrariness of the sign gives way to an idea of 'trace-structure', as Gayatri Spivak calls it. 'The structure of the sign', she writes, 'is determined by the trace or track of that other which is forever absent' ('Preface', p. xvii).

Now this of course is what writing in the narrow sense is said to have instituted. As written-down speech, writing is condemned to open the way to absence – the absence of the one who wrote and the absence of the thing itself that was written about. In Derrida's words, writing 'constitutes the absence of the signatory, to say nothing of the absence of the referent. Writing is the name of these two absences' (OG, 40–1). *Writing marks the loss of presence. Writing institutes the trace-structure of meaning.* But this is true to the extent only that writing is confined to mean phonetic writing, written-down speech, a secondary system of representation substituting for an originary mode of communication. As Derrida sees it, though, it is in fact a generalized writing (tracing in general) that opens the way to a distinction between speech-as-presence and writing-as-representation. 'If "writing" signifies inscription and especially the durable institution of a sign (and that is the only irreducible kernel of the concept of writing), writing in general covers the entire field of linguistic signs' (OG, 45). This is to say that no sign contains the thing itself within it; what every sign 'contains' is the absence of a referent, the non-presence of the thing it refers to, the thing of which it is a sign. Regardless of being spoken or written, every sign is an instituted trace, a mark or inscription of 'that other which is forever absent'. Whether I were to say or to write the word 'apple', I would be using a sign. Even if I stuck an apple in my mouth and pointed to it I would be using a sign, and *as a sign* my gesture would be separated from its referent. No matter what technology or technique is used to signify 'apple', the signification will depend on the absence of the apple as such. Every conceivable form of the sign 'apple' (spoken, written, drawn, photographed, computerized) must not *be* an apple. Such is the trace-structure of the sign. It is not only so-called written signs but all signs that are conditioned by the absence of the other, of the thing or referent that *is not there* within the sign except as the trace or inference of a former presence that can never be restored or made to come back.

The non-presence of the referent, then, is not a special kind of loss belonging only to writing in the narrow sense, but certainly the absence of the referent has been seen traditionally as one of the defining features of that writing. Its other defining feature – 'the absence of the signatory' – may seem to mount a stronger case for regarding writing as distinctly different from speech. Yet this feature too belongs to writing in general and not simply to phonetic writing, written-down speech or writing as representation. Let's put aside for a moment the question of the recorded voice in order to suppose that for you to hear me speak, you and I have to be in each other's presence. I have to be present to speak, you have to be present to listen. By contrast I don't have to be present for you to read something I might have written (like this book). Now while this is true, the problem is that it makes it seem that the presence of a sign-user is essential to speech and incidental to writing. From this it follows that the absence or the non-presence of the signatory is a condition of writing only, and it may follow from this that writing is less reliable or less authentic than speech. But if we go back to the founding assumption (the sign-user's presence is essential to speech) we might find that it can be sustained only if we disregard everything we know about the sign, everything that Saussure could be said to have taught us. The presence of a subject, in other words, is entirely incidental to sign usage. The structure of the sign owes nothing to the structure-as-presence of the subject. Not only, moreover, is the subject's presence merely incidental; the very thesis of the arbitrariness of the sign makes this a necessity. For signs to be signs, for signs to circulate or be exchanged within a sign-using community, it is necessary that they signify in the absence of subjects and in the absence of referents. Yes, when I speak a sign I do so according to a technique that is different from the technique I would use to write a sign. This is to acknowledge that speech and writing have their particularities, they have their differences. You would have to be the Van Morrison of fruitcakes to think they don't. All the same the different particularities of speech and writing cannot be reduced to the difference between speech-as-presence and writing-as-representation, or between speech-as-presence and writing-as-absence – *presence* of subject and referent in speech, *non-presence* of subject and referent in writing, etc. 'The very idea of institution', Derrida writes '– hence of the arbitrariness of the sign – is unthinkable before the possibility of writing outside of its horizon.' Indeed it is unthinkable 'outside of the horizon itself', which is to say 'outside the world as space of inscription, as the opening to the emission and to the spatial *distribution* of signs, to the *regulated play* of their differences, even if they are "phonic"' (OG, 44).

Even 'phonic' signs are inside the structure of a general writing, inside 'the world as space of *inscription*'. The spoken sign has its particularities, but it does not contain a presence that is absent from the written sign. Because absence is associated historically with writing in the narrow sense, however, Derrida refers to the condition of every sign's possibility as that of *writing in general* (or what he sometimes calls the arche-trace). It is this general writing that must come before the sign, inhabiting and enervating the trace-structure of every signifier–signified relationship. Such a writing – a writing of the trace – both makes signification possible and makes it impossible to get outside of signification to an unmediated, non-representational, uncontextual, transcendental presence.

This does not lead to relativism, and it does not necessitate that we can never know what anything means. We know, for instance, that when James Brown sings about a 'sex machine' he isn't referring to a dildo, and we get the joke when Iggy Pop sings the line (from 'Nazi Girlfriend'), 'Her French is perfect, so's her butt'. But there is nothing within language or signification that determines those meanings or effects; indeed it is the lack of any structural determination (or the force of structural indeterminacy) that makes innuendo, ambiguity, figuration and the like possible. Precisely because of the lack of any necessary relation between linguistic and physical 'perfection', it is possible to draw or trace a relation between being fluent in French and having a cute ass (*un cul coquet*). But, as with any tracing, the relation that emerges is impermanent, barely perceptible, utterly contextual. What might be called the 'being-there' of the trace, in other words, satisfies only the very least ontological or the most minimal condition of 'being' anything at all. So the point of Derrida's insistence on rethinking the sign in terms of the trace is to de-ontologize presence, as it were, or to make presence as inert, ineffectual, undetermined and undetermining as can be. For it is not possible to get rid of presence altogether, or to get outside of metaphysics. All that can be done is to denounce, at every opportunity, the metaphysical power and authority of presence, in the name of **justice** and **democracy** to come, in the name of every 'forever absent' other that presence excludes.

Barely discernible, the trace is barely ontological; it is almost not quite there. Is a broken twig a sign or just a broken twig? ('Is that a gun in your pocket', as Mae West is said to have quipped famously to a young man who approached her at a party, 'or are you just happy to see me?') In its almost-not-quite-there-ness, then, the trace cannot be seen to begin as an already constituted unit of signification: its ontology remains putative and circumstantial, raising the question of how to distinguish (say) between a typographical error and a neologism (**differance** being the obvious case in point here). Simply to posit a trace is to bring it into 'the world as space of inscription', or to bring it into a condition of interpretative activity. All those fabulous sunglasses in Godard's *Breathless* (1959): are they a sign of something (a glamorous surface concealing the 'true identity' of characters in the film?) or just so much incidental dross, a more or less 'non-signifying' replication of the state of fashion outside the text? Or when (in 1672) Dryden argued in his 'Defence of the Epilogue' that the literature of his own age was superior to that of Shakespeare and his contemporaries, claiming that 'our improprieties are less frequent, and less gross than theirs' ('Defence', 87) – should this be taken for a sign of his disinterested aesthetic judgement or as a trace of Dryden's allegiance to the newly re-established Crown, which together with his fellow Tories he believed responsible for bringing greater freedom to English life and art? After all, only a few months before Charles's restoration in 1660, in a pamphlet whose full title appeared originally as 'The Readie & Easy Way to Establish a Free Commonwealth, and the Excellence thereof compar'd with the inconveniences and dangers of readmitting kingship in this nation', Milton had sought to warn his countrymen against the impending **spectre** of reinstated monarchy, or what he called 'this noxious humour of returning to bondage, instill'd of late by some deceivers, and nourished from bad principles and fals apprehensions among too many of the people' ('Readie and Easy', 327). So clearly there is room for disagreement, even among great artists, concerning the question of what constitutes good government, if not also great art, and surely there could be no hope of resolving that disagreement by deference simply to 'already constituted units of signification'. Indeed it is the structural indeterminacy of the sign – its lack of an already constituted 'unity'– coupled with the lack of recognition of this fact, that leads to differences of opinion regarding the quality and substance of aesthetic and other forms of judgement. A judgement always has to be made in response to a particular set of circumstances, even when it is invoked as a transcendental rule. There is no outside-context, as it were. But the failure to acknowledge the stubborn contextuality of every judgement produces the idea that texts belong within the determination of presence, as if it were only in rare or special cases that we might have occasion to worry over the nature of a text's identity.

This is why confusion arises sometimes over the question of how to judge a text that appears to belong 'outside' genre, for example, such as James Hogg's *The Private Memoirs and Confessions of a Justified Sinner* (1824) and Melville's *The Confidence-Man* (1857) – or (at the time of their release) Elvis's early records.

If, however, the speech–writing opposition actually did come after the speech–writing succession there would be no confusion or disagreement over anything – since in fact there would be nothing to judge. Everything would be (and mean) within the time and place allotted to it by metaphysics. But Derrida's argument – crucial to any conception or estimation of deconstruction – is that the disseminatory, spatial and distributive effects of a general writing must come before the possibility of thinking that any text, let alone every text, is grounded in presence, and it must do so as the condition of that possibility. This is to acknowledge that the speech–writing opposition is already 'in' deconstruction; it is not the case that Derrida imposes a deconstruction on it from somewhere outside the trace-structure of that opposition 'itself'. But of course to accept that the speech–writing opposition begins in deconstruction is to accept Derrida's argument that it does so, which is to admit that his account of the relations between speech and writing constitutes a position, a particular take on the nature of those relations. The contexts and the consequences of deconstruction, as it were, can never be separated. Should this be taken as a 'first principle' of deconstruction, it should not be taken to mean therefore that deconstruction contradicts itself by holding to such a principle, or even by holding to anything like principles at all.

Nor should it be supposed that Derrida got out of bed one morning and, just like that, all on his own, thought up the quasi-transcendental principle that there is no outside-context. He did at least have a bit of help – from the likes of **Freud** and **Nietzsche**, among others. In Freud's discussion of neurosis, for example, he makes it clear that context is everything, or at any rate that a neurosis is not a condition with an undivided presence of its own. It comes into being only in the interval or gap between an infantile experience and a 'triggering' adult event that bears no determined or necessary relation to that experience. Indeed not even the experience itself has a necessary presence (or a necessarily former presence), since it makes no difference to Freud whether the infantile experience is real or conjured (see *Lectures*). What matters is that the actual or virtual infantile experience and the undetermined adult event come together in a context, forming a supplementary series of contingent elements whose meaning is the effect of a differential relation. 'Both of these [the infantile experience and the adult event] are needed for the neurosis', writes Tony Thwaites, summarizing the argument nicely: 'without the latter, the former remains invisible, unproblematic; and without the former, the latter is merely transient and without lasting effect' (*Temporalities*, 52). From this we might be able to see a certain association with Derrida's discussion of the speech–writing opposition, in so far as one of the consequences of Freud's argument is that we cannot think of a neurosis in terms of a 'secondary' or 'exterior' condition that befalls subjectivity and thereafter contaminates it from 'within'. More generally, of course, Freud's theory of the unconscious as a kind of non-present, 'groundless ground' of subjectivity helps us to see the other within the self, as it were, such that the very notion of subjectivity is put 'under erasure' (*sous rature*) by the work of the unconscious.

'Under erasure' refers to a practice of **Heidegger**'s which Derrida employed sparingly in the past but seems to have abandoned, no doubt because what it can be taken to signify is too easily mistaken for a 'trick' or a 'gimmick' which can be used to trivialize deconstruction (*deconstruction stands for the cancellation or impossibility of meaning* – and other such benighted nonsense). It refers to the practice of crossing out certain words (key metaphysical concepts) that have to be used ('being', 'is', etc.), because it is not possible to think and write outside of metaphysics altogether, even though Derrida was seeking to denounce their authority and presence. Like the term *differance*, the inscriptive practice of putting a word under erasure (<being *with superimposed 'cross-out'*>, <is *with superimposed 'cross-out'*>, etc.) has no speech equivalent; it cannot be translated into, and certainly it cannot be translated 'back' into, speech. In so far as it operates purely as a writing effect it helps to undermine the notion that signs originate in spoken language and contradicts the standard definition of writing as a secondary system of signification. So to let 'being' appear in 'itself' and in its cancellation serves to show the dividedness of being, which denies both the presence of being and that presence is an undeconstructible ground of identity or truth. Freud elaborates a similar notion of 'self-divided being' (or the non-self-identity of the subject) in his insistence on the necessary separation of the psyche and the psychic apparatus, the operations of the latter being forever inaccessible to the psyche as such. Once again there is a relation here to the deconstruction of the speech–writing opposition, especially in Freud's choice of a 'mystic writing-pad' as a figure of the psychic apparatus (see 'Note'). The mysterious writing pad in question refers to a child's toy consisting of a stylus and a sheet of waxed paper over a wooden board; the paper is 'cleaned' by lifting it, leaving any markings that were made on it to remain as permanent but almost imperceptible traces or imprints. This, for Freud, is how the apparatus of the psyche operates, unbeknown to the psychic self. Here the trace-structure of the unconscious exceeds the notion of a 'secondary' or 'derivative' effect of an originating consciousness and is described instead in terms of a necessarily generative *supplementarity* that belongs to writing. The radical otherness of the unconscious, then, puts under erasure 'the self' as consciously present to itself. 'The alterity of the "unconscious"', Derrida writes, 'makes us concerned not with horizons of modified – past or future – presents, but with a "past" that has never been present, whose future to come will never be a *production* or a reproduction in the form of presence' (MoP, 21). So for all that Derrida may be critical of the 'scientific' aspirations of psychoanalysis, what he sees in Freud's positive depiction of the *inscriptive* nature of the unconscious is a way of understanding writing which does not rely on having to oppose it to speech.

In Nietzsche, too, Derrida sees possibilities for thinking otherwise about the nature of writing. What Nietzsche calls 'will to power' is expressed as a need to acquire knowledge of the world, which is really a need to conquer or to have power over it. But Nietzsche's 'knowledge' does not equate with absolute truth; on the contrary it consists only of active interpretations of the world, undertaken out of fear of chaos. Knowledge, then, orders the disorder of things, such that order appears only as an effect of figuration, interpretation, metaphoricity – writing. This is why Nietzsche's writing (in the literal sense) is so stylish and stylistically multivalent: rhetorical excess is an affirmation of the empirical play of differences that every science, philosophy or knowledge of the world tries to bring under the sway of a sort of 'non-metaphorical' or 'degree zero' system of representation, a kind of speech-equivalent writing. And so with Nietzsche we get, as Derrida puts it, an 'entire thematics of active interpretations, which substitutes an incessant deciphering for the disclosure of truth as a presentation of the thing itself' (SP, 149). Such 'incessant deciphering' is not simply a wild take on knowledge as will to power, for knowledge alone is not enough according to Nietzsche: we need also to cultivate the will to ignorance (see *Will*). 'We are unknown to ourselves, we men of knowledge', he writes, '– and with good reason. We have never sought ourselves – how could it happen that we should ever *find* ourselves?' (*Genealogy*, 15). We are unknown to ourselves, that is to say, *because* we are men of

knowledge. Or we're unknown to ourselves because we are men of knowledge and *not* men of ignorance. Will to ignorance ('gay science' or 'joyful
wisdom') opens itself to uncertainty, to the chance- or trace-like structure
of the disorder of things as they are, a sort of structure-without-structure
that can never be revealed in 'the disclosure of truth as a presentation of
the thing itself'.

So it could be said that Nietzsche unleashes the will to ignorance in
his assault on the philosophical tradition's 'conspiratorial' suppression of
metaphor. In order to remember or memorialize the concept, philosophy
forgets the figure. Nietzsche, though, forgets to remember the philosophically correct order of this succession and hence exploits the resources of
writing in the name of doing philosophy. Puns, 'poetic' turns of phrase,
modal shifts, altered registers, stylistic heterogeneity, generic variegation –
everything philosophy excludes, Nietzsche puts in. The exuberance with
which he seems to pull devices out of his ragbag of rhetorical tricks,
indeed, could even be characterized as mad or hysterical – conditions he
associates with women, or at any rate with the figure of 'woman'. This is
the source of his infamous (alleged) misogyny. But, as Derrida argues in
*Spurs*, madness, irrationality, hysteria, excess, experimentation: these are
all positives for Nietzsche, who associates them with style and writing and
exploits their effects in the war against the philosophical conception of
'truth as a presentation of the thing itself'. Moreover throughout Nietzsche's
writing *woman* herself (or itself) is associated with notions of writing and
metaphoricity, and with the kind of truth that philosophical reason could
never know (truth 'under erasure', perhaps). Both woman and writing,
then, are associated in Nietzsche 'with everything that beguiles, seduces
or perverts the mastery of philosophic concepts', as Christopher Norris
remarks (*Derrida*, 203). Clearly this does not mean that Nietzsche was
really a closet feminist who was forced by the misogynistic times in which
he wrote to express his solidarity with women only in code. But it does
suggest that to presume to know unequivocally the truth of Nietzsche's
'hatred' towards women would involve having to ignore everything he
wrote about knowledge, truth, woman and writing. This would be to
see his published work merely as the secondary representation (or as the
'translation') of Nietzsche's originary intentions, as though in spite of
everything philosophy must always continue to assert its mastery over the
text. It would be to see his writing only as written-down speech and not
as writing at all. (See also ARTIFACTUALITY, ITERABILITY, *PHARMAKON*,
PHONOCENTRISM, POSTAL METAPHOR, VIRTUALITY.)

**structure**  Very broadly, on Derrida's account in the essay 'Structure, Sign, and **Play** in the Discourse of the Human Sciences', the concept of structure has been thought of in two ways, corrresponding (very roughly) to two historical phases. Before **Nietzsche** – going all the way back to **Plato** – structure was conceptualized in terms of 'a center' or by 'referring it to a point of **presence**, a fixed **origin**' (WD, 278). Following Nietzsche's critique of the **metaphysics** of truth (and then **Freud**'s of the metaphysics of the self, **Heidegger**'s of the metaphysics of presence – the list is partial; the 'history' potted), the 'earlier' concept of structure gave way, slowly and without organization, to a new or modified concept of *decentred* structure that came to be associated with what became known as structuralism. In terms of disciplinary or institutional influence, the two most important figures in the formation of this 'new' concept of 'decentred' structure are **Saussure** and Lévi-Strauss. While Derrida begs to differ differently with these two figures, it may be said that his general problem with the structuralist version of structure is that it remains, despite appearances and affirmations to the contrary, an all too familiar metaphysics. So the structuralist concept of decentred or even, as it were, 'structureless' structure is not the same as the 'Platonic' version of structure, but neither is it wholly different.

For structuralism, any differences between say Platonic structure and Nietzschean structure would be effects of a larger system of structural differences, whether in the form of Lévi-Strauss's structure of 'the' human mind or Saussure's *langue* as a rule-governing system of differential relations. On this model the difference between 'centred' and 'decentred' structure (or between any binary opposition) is generated from an overarching or underlying structure of differences between 'nonpositive' terms (Saussure, *Course*, 120). There is no question that this represents an attempt at thinking 'difference' differently, outside the limits of a 'pure' or 'natural' occurrence between things in themselves (as originary moments or ahistorical **events**, for example). No doubt this is what lent structuralism its 'scientific' appeal, leading also to much controversy (see Lucy, 'Structuralism'). Yet for all that structuralism thinks past nature as the bedrock on which differences are grounded, it cannot let go of an idea that differences must be grounded on something, that there must be something underpinning differences which in itself is centred and centring – in a word, full of presence. For structuralism, of course, that something is *structure*. So it may be said that structuralism remains, after all, a familiar metaphysics, because it fails to ask the question, *What is the structure of* *structure?* Or, which amounts to the same, it never asks after the 'structure' of presence.

This – an uncritical adherence to the 'anteriority' of presence – shows through for instance in Saussure's repetition of the standard conception of **writing** as a **suppplement** to speech. In Saussure's words, speech and writing are 'two distinct systems of signs; the second *exists for the sole purpose of representing* the first' (cited in OG, 30). As with Rousseau, spoken language is primary and natural for Saussure, who treats writing as a kind of costume or *parergon* which, in representing speech, also misrepresents it: 'Writing veils the appearance of language; it is not a guise for language but a disguise' (cited in OG, 35). The structure of Saussure's version of the **speech–writing opposition** is determined therefore by the originary structure of 'the natural bond' located in the indivisible unity of sense and sound, or between signified and *phonic* signifier. But for the structure of the spoken sign to be 'non-representational' (indivisibly prior and natural), writing *has* to be put on the side of 'the post' (determined by, derived from, secondary to), as something that comes after speech only to (mis)represent it. Yet the structure of this opposition never quite works as Saussure (and many others, including Rousseau and Plato) would ideally like it to work. The trouble lies in associating speech with presence and writing with re-presentation. This of course makes it look as though speech comes first. In so far as writing could be said to be representation's first name, however, then in fact writing must come before speech, since it is only from within representation (within 'writing') that it is possible to conceive of something (especially something representational, like speech) as 'non-representational'. Note that this argument has nothing to do with historical developments concerning language; its focus is the less than ideally stable or determining structure of a crucial opposition.

On Saussure's own account, the relationship between any signifier and signified (we need not go into the exceptions here) is 'unmotivated' or 'arbitrary'. The structure of the sign is such that there is no 'natural attachment' between signifier and signified. As Derrida remarks, however, this 'puts in question the idea of naturalness rather than that of attachment' (OG, 46). For surely a sign that consisted of a natural attachment between a signifier and a signified would not be a sign at all; in its naturalness it would be a 'representation' that was non-representational, a contradiction in terms. Such a 'sign' could be only a 'transcendental signified', the very thing in itself that could exist only outside of all signs, all representation, all writing. Yet such existence could be posited or felt only from within what Derrida refers to as 'the general possibility of writing' on which the possibility of equating natural language with speech depends (OG, 52). Writing, then, as a name for what might be called representation in general, conditions the structure of the opposition between speech and writing. This is to say that writing structures that opposition. But it also unstructures it at the same time, because writing comes before speech and hence before the structure of its opposition to speech as a supplementary or representational form of the original.

What is a structure that performs a double movement of structuring and unstructuring at once? Perhaps it could be called a *structure without structure*, or at least without the traditional effects of structure in the form of an indivisible bonding or binding between one thing and another. Without quite acknowledging it, Saussure himself saw (or could have seen) that structure does in fact perform a 'double' operation, for what else is the unmotivated attachment of signifier and signified but a perfect example of the double movement of structure at work? Precisely because of the doubling effects of the structure of the sign, Saussure could argue that signifieds are held within signification, fully inscribed within a signifying system that produces (or *represents*) them as coming first, as though they existed prior to and outside of signification or 'the general possibility of writing'. Or indeed outside of signification *as* the general possibility of writing, or vice versa.

For Saussure, then, and for structuralism generally, all differences are grounded on a determining *structure* of difference. While this dislocates or decentres the idea that differences are natural, transcendental or innate, it does not otherwise disturb metaphysics. This is the lesson of 'Structure, Sign, and Play', which Derrida delivered in 1967 to a conference at Johns Hopkins University which was intended to mark the arrival of structuralism in the United States. The focus here is on Lévi-Strauss's distinction between *bricolage* and engineering discourse, where the former describes an asystematic or creative approach to meaning, such that the meaning of a cultural practice or a literary **text** is produced unpremeditatedly, by making use of whatever happens to be at hand in order to see what 'works'. By contrast, engineering (or scientific) discourse proceeds according to unvarying rules and inflexible methods of analysis that enable the engineer or the scientist to solve a problem not by trial and error, but through the rigorous application of rational thought. In this way the engineer or the scientist appears to be the author of his own discourse, sole progenitor of an idea, a theory or a solution. As Derrida argues, though, this distinction

between creative and rational thinking depends on a structure of determination that separates them by putting rationality first and relegating
creativity to the order of a special or supplementary case. Yet if *bricolage*,
as a form of creative thought in general, is characterized by the necessity of
borrowing ideas and concepts from a general history of ideas, then surely
*bricolage* is typical of every discourse. In that case the absolutely uncreative
rationality of the engineer is a 'myth' created by *bricolage* (WD, 285).

Once again the structure of difference – here between *bricolage* and
engineering discourse (or creative and rational thought) – turns out to
move in two directions at the same time. Lévi-Strauss himself glimpsed
this double movement in what he called the 'scandal' of the incest prohibition, but only to turn away from it. The 'scandal' comes from recognizing
that every culture prohibits incest (hence the prohibition is universal,
belonging on the side of nature), yet the prohibition itself (as a prohibition or a rule) is cultural. In this way the incest prohibition scandalizes the
difference between nature and culture, a difference that has always been
taken for granted in 'the domain of traditional concepts' (WD, 283). It is
that whole domain of thought, then, the domain of metaphysics, and not
simply the structure of the nature–culture opposition, which is scandalized
by the incest prohibition: the structure of the incest prohibition cannot be
thought within the structure of metaphysics. The very *scandalous* structure
of that prohibition both exceeds and precedes the formation of traditional
concepts – as 'the condition of their possibility' (WD, 283) and therefore
as the condition of possibility for the metaphysical structure of structure.
So it turns out that the 'scandalous' difference of the nature–culture
opposition comes before the conceptualization of any *structural* or *metaphysical* difference between nature and culture. This is to say that the
scandal runs very deep. 'It could perhaps be said that the whole of philosophical conceptualization, which is systematic with the nature/culture
opposition, is designed to leave in the domain of the unthinkable the very
thing that makes this conceptualization possible: the **origin** of the prohibition of incest' (WD, 283–4).

In its double movement, the incest prohibition (natural because
universal, cultural because prohibitive) scandalizes metaphysics. In its
**undecidability**, the structure of the prohibition cannot be understood in
terms of a centre or an origin. Derrida's point is that this undecidability
– the undecidable structure of the incest prohibition, or *the structure of
undecidability* – is what conditions the possibility of concepts such as
'centre' and 'origin'. Centres and origins are never just there from the

beginning, in other words; rather than preceding the work of undecidability, they proceed from it. This is to repeat the argument that writing must come before the structure of its opposition to speech. Similarly, culture must come before the structure of its opposition to nature. Such an argument is a 'scandal' only from within the field of metaphysics, where structure's double movement is concealed by the idea that structure is foundational and therefore undeconstructible. But what in fact opens the structure or the structurality of structure to the possibility of being deconstructed is an opening or movement within structure itself. In its double movement, structure shows that it contains a certain degree of 'give' or 'play', just as there is always movement in the most tightly bolted engine or the tautest length of rope. This 'movement of play', as Derrida terms it, is 'the movement of *supplementarity*' (WD, 289), which is the condition of possibility that structures every opposition. The structurality of structure is therefore supplementary. This is not to say that we should henceforth reject or that we could ever abandon structure as a word or a concept. 'There is no sense', Derrida reminds us, 'in doing without the concepts of metaphysics in order to shake metaphysics. We have no language – no syntax and no lexicon – which is foreign to this history' (WD, 280). **Deconstruction** is not anti-metaphysical, then, and neither is poststructuralism anti-structuralist. The purpose of Derrida's poststructuralist rethinking of the metaphysical concept of structure is to show that that concept, like any concept, depends on the necessity of **presence** being seen as undeconstructible. Metaphysics depends on this necessity, a necessity which occludes its own dependence on the movement of supplementarity (the play of and within structure), which explains why deconstruction commits itself to showing that presence is always deconstructible and must – for critical, political and many other reasons – always be deconstructed. (See also APORIA, BEING, DIFFERANCE, IDENTITY, ITERABILITY, LOGOCENTRISM, PROPER, TEXT.)

**supplementarity**    It is probably not often that thought has taken a path from **Kant** to a G-string, but Derrida has gone down that way at least once (TP, 57). The occasion is his lengthy meditation on Kant's use of the term *parergon* in *The Critique of Judgement*, referring to something that is both ornamental to and which augments a beautiful form. A picture frame, for instance, can work in both of these ways: to ornament and to augment the beauty of the painting it frames. If a frame were merely ornamental (leaving aside for now the question of how to judge the distinction), it would be but a piece of 'finery' and therefore not parergonal. Kant's other example is the drapery on statues, where the clothes can be seen to adorn and complement a statue's beauty. But, as Derrida notes, Kant is clear on the *parergon* being always outside and inessential 'to the total representation of the object' (TP, 57), belonging to it 'only in an extrinsic way' (ibid.) as a kind of comely adjunct to the already fully constituted beauty of the object itself. Here's where the question of judgement arises: what distinguishes *parerga* from mere finery if, after all, the beauty of a beautiful thing is already complete? How could something complete in itself, full of plenitude and **presence**, abundant with 'total representation', be augmented? How is it possible to add something to what is already *total*? In the same vein, one could ask where *parerga* begin and end. What should we make of the naked Lucretia, in the painting by the German artist Lucas Cranach (1472–1553), who 'holds only a light band of transparent veil in front of her sex' (TP, 57)? Is the veil a *parergon*? Is any garment parergonal – 'G-strings and the like' (ibid.)?

What these questions illustrate is the less than total 'totality' of Kant's conception of the object; more to the point they illustrate the necessity of Kant's unacknowledged conception of the object's 'incomplete' totality. Elsewhere – in a reading not of Kant but of Rousseau – Derrida identifies this same necessity as the logic or 'strange economy' of the supplement (OG, 154), or simply *supplementarity*. So we can say here that the relations between parergonality and supplementarity are, in a word, supplementary.

To see what this might mean we need to return momentarily to Kant, who made a strong case for acknowledging the 'purity' of reason and beauty. Strong, but not impervious. For what Kant's references to the *parergon* show, Derrida argues, is that the very idea of purity or 'naturalness' turns out to contain its opposite. This is the necessary sense in which every so-called pure object (or pure concept) requires supplementation. Say for instance that the definition of the purity of a work of art were given as *the totality of its representation*, where 'totality' describes everything internal to the work, everything inside the field of its pure beauty (or its beautiful purity). What would be the limits of this field? What could be used to mark the distinction between what is inside the work (which is the work itself) and everything external to it? For Kant, the purity of the work can be augmented – supplemented – by things that belong to it only provisionally, tentatively, inessentially, since they remain strictly outside it. Yet still they augment its 'purity', a purity that must therefore have been always less than pure from the start. From the beginning, then, the original purity of the work of art contains a *lack*. It is this lack (an originary lack) that the supplement supplements.

So the work of supplementarity turns out to be essential to the constitution of 'the work itself'. Essential, but also threatening, because it reveals that without the supplement there *is* no 'itself' of the work. The very idea of the work itself is constituted only *in the work of supplementarity*, so that the difference between 'inside' and 'outside' the work is rendered **undecidable**. What seems to be the defining characteristic of the supplement, moreover, namely that it can be detached or dispensed with (like a G-string or a painted veil – or, as we shall see in a moment, like television), makes it not less but all the more necessary to the work it performs in helping to constitute an idea of the object (as art work, the human body, human **being**, human culture, etc.) in terms of its own originary completion. Derrida refers therefore to the supplement's 'quasi-detachment', without which 'the lack on the inside of the work would appear, or (which amounts to the same thing for a lack) would not appear' (TP, 59). This has many important implications. In terms of contemporary understandings of culture, for example, one could say that television is indeed culture's supplement, and this would mean something very different (of a critical and political nature) from standard put-downs of the media, backed up usually with the authority of some psychological study or pronouncement. In performing the work of supplementarity, television need not be regarded – on the contrary – as interfering with the work of culture. As culture's G-string, television is often seen as dangerously seductive, salacious and distracting – of the order of an illicit pleasure which, through over-indulgence, can lead one astray from the path of hard work, right-mindedness and goodwill to others. But it may be that 'the dangerous supplement' of television is not in fact to blame for alleged increases in urban crime rates, poor literacy among the young or the destruction of 'family values'.

In any case, television is a latecomer to the list of culture's 'dangerous' supplements. As Derrida shows in a reading of Rousseau, supplementarity is thought to begin its dangerous work with the invention of **writing**! Like Kant, Rousseau held to a certain ideal of originary purity, which for him could be located in an authentic language of the passions and instincts. This 'natural' language however has been lost to us, signalling 'the degeneracy of culture and the disruption of the community' (OG, 144). On Rousseau's account, all that is pure, essential and authentic belongs on the side of nature, compared to which all cultural experiences, practices, technologies and the like are second-rate. Writing, then, as a 'secondary' form of communication, a 'substitute' for the natural (spoken) language of the passions, alienates us from the 'truth' of our 'authentic' being. As Rousseau puts it, 'writing serves only as a supplement to speech' – and this endangers truth because 'the art of writing is nothing but a mediated representation of thought' (cited in OG, 144). Truth and thought, in other words, are present to one another in the human voice; the natural language of speech, the originary medium of communication, guarantees that the intended meaning is precisely what is said. In writing, that guarantee is lost, due to its second-order status as only a 'mediated' form of representation. This means of course that speech – in its 'natural' state, as Rousseau imagines 'it should be or rather as it *should have been*' (OG, 141) – has the status of unmediated representation, full of purity and presence.

As a supplement to speech, writing plays two roles (or a double role). In a positive sense, it can be said to augment speech by extending it across historical and geographical distances. Negatively, though, because the 'thing itself' is never actually there in writing, it can be said that writing tries to pass itself off as the thing itself. In writing, lies may parade as the truth, even though writing has the potential to disseminate the truth more widely than speech. Defined simply as written-down speech, writing must always be less than what it copies, even though, as a technology for copying the truth, writing can lead to good effects.

In these paradoxical roles (this double role), writing is typical of every supplement, which always 'harbours within itself two significations whose cohabitation is as strange as it is necessary' (OG, 144). Every supplement (be it writing or a G-string) adds something; 'it is a surplus, a plenitude enriching another plenitude' (ibid.). Writing adds to speech the capacity further to disseminate truth; a G-string adds eroticism to the body. But the supplement 'adds only to replace. It intervenes or insinuates itself *in-the-place-of*' (OG, 145). Writing takes the place of speech; the G-string takes the place of sexual organs. Like Kant's *parergon*, Rousseau's supplement is always on the outside looking in: 'whether it adds or substitutes itself, the supplement is *exterior*, outside of the positivity to which it is super-added, alien to that which, in order to be replaced by it, must be other than it' (ibid.).

Once again, the problem of **inside–outside** relations appears. For writing to be exterior to speech, speech must be self-sufficient (filled with 'positivity') and entirely other than writing. In this it is defined by its proximity to truth, to things in themselves. Yet regardless of being spoken or written, the sign 'tree' is not a tree; it's a sign, a representation. As representation, it is also always already a mediation. Spoken words, no less than images on television, are media. Writing is no more a technology of communication than speech.

As media, speech and writing both conform to 'the logic of the supplement'. Like television, they conjoin in a process of 'ineluctably multiplying the supplementary mediations that produce the sense of the very thing they defer: the mirage of the thing itself' (OG, 157). While it is true that the thing itself can never be found in writing, the point is that neither can it be found inside representation generally (speech, music, television, painting, sign language and so on), and every representation is a system (of sorts) of 'supplementary mediations'. The further point is that there is no chance of getting outside of representation *to* the thing itself, the very idea of which (both the idea that there might be a chance and the idea of the thing itself) is something that representations 'produce'. This would not be to deny that we experience the world in terms of real **events** and objects, on the basis of a **metaphysics** that instils a strong sense of the dividing line between the inside and the outside of a thing. Yet it is from within metaphysics that this sense is given to us and within which our experience of 'experience', as it were, is held. So if it were to be shown that the order of relations between things does not quite match the metaphysical ideal, surely this would be of consequence. In teasing out the 'double' logic of supplementarity, then, showing that it works both to add and to substitute at the same time, Derrida's purpose is not simply to outdo Kant and Rousseau. The purpose is not reducible simply to an effort to do philosophy 'better' than the likes of them (and others), or to provide philosophy with 'better' ways of thinking about the 'nature' of things. Instead, if the very nature of things – the very idea of nature itself and therefore of **identity**, essence, **origin** and so forth – turned out to depend on something other than the absolute self-sufficiency of things themselves, the consequences could never be confined to philosophy as such. Nor could they be contained within the purview of 'abstract thought', 'disinterested analysis' and other variations on a derogatory idea of academicism as a mere supplement to real life. They would have, for instance, political consequences. For how could something like an idea of the inviolability of national borders be sustained in light of the argument that originary concepts such as 'nation', on which ideas of national identity and sovereignty are founded, thereby justifying the protection of national borders, are unsustainable?

Who would have thought reflecting on a G-string could bring us to this? But what the detour – this entry as a **text** of 'supplementary mediations' – might help to show is that one of the lessons of **deconstruction** involves having to think against the limits of a metaphysics in which there is a place for everything and everything has its place. While there is no question that sometimes a G-string is just a G-string (in the way that every nation does have an identity), nevertheless a G-string isn't reducible to the function of a 'sex aid'; it can also be a philosophical concept, or at any rate an occasion for thought, as defined by metaphysics, to 'stray' in unexpected and productive ways. This does not mean that deconstruction claims to be outside of metaphysics or to run counter to it. The point of Derrida's detailed readings of Kant and Rousseau (a point that is not 'merely' philosophical but also ethico-political), produced out of his attention to those philosophers' infrequent and seemingly insignificant uses of the terms *parergon* and 'supplement', is that metaphysical arguments (which are also political arguments) cannot sustain themselves. Metaphysical categories (which are also political categories) of the origin, the essence, the identity, etc. of $X$ require supplementation. Every originary $X$ is in need of supplementation by what is other-than-$X$, such that nothing short of 'an infinite chain' (OG, 157) of relations between $X$ and its others leads to the very 'mirage' of $X$ being self-sufficient, the idea of $X$ 'itself'. This holds, on Derrida's account, regardless of whether $X$ is taken philosophically, politically or in some other way. It also holds, of course, for the categories of 'philosophy' and 'politics' themselves, each of them having an identity that is never less than supplementary through and through. (See also ARTIFACTUALITY, DIFFERANCE, ITERABILITY, POSTAL METAPHOR, *PHARMAKON*, SPEECH–WRITING OPPOSITION, SPECTRALITY, STRUCTURE, TRACE, VIRTUALITY.)

**teletechnology**     Derrida uses 'teletechnology' in association usually with the media, where 'the media' is shorthand for several 'tele-' effects and operations: 'tele-communications, techno-tele-discursivity, techno-tele-iconicity' (SoM, 51). In one sense all technology is of the order of the 'tele-' (meaning 'distance') for Derrida, inasmuch as **metaphysics** opposes technology to **presence** in the form of 'nature'; hence technology is said to put us at a distance from ourselves, or to alienate us from a **proper** sense of **being**. This is not Derrida's position regarding technology, of course, but neither is it his position that technologies do not have any effects at all.

Any opposition along the lines of technology versus nature would be a form of the **speech–writing opposition**, though again this doesn't mean that particular technologies do not have particular effects and operations. In the case of teletechnology, its particular effects are bound up historically with technological developments that have reduced the time it takes to send 'information' and extended the distance over which it is possible to circulate it. Such developments have led to a 'new' experience of communication which appears to de-ontologize time and space. If this evokes an idea of the 'virtual', it doesn't do so at the expense of all considerations of the real. As a medium for the production of the virtual, teletechnology may produce unwanted effects. But it is also a potentially democratizing force that can be used, as McKenzie Wark argues, 'to create a people aware of its capacity to produce itself as a people' ('Too Real', 161). Such a people would not possess a sense of 'virtual **identity**' in opposition to a former sense of 'true nature'. On the contrary, it would be a people 'aware of its potential, of the things it can make of itself, the things it can do and be' (ibid.).

It is important to stress that since there has never been a time when the circulation of information was confined to face-to-face or person-to-person contact, then there was never any time at which it could be said that technology arrived within culture to 'displace' some sort of **original** and authentic mode of communication. But certainly the invention of digital technologies and satellite communications systems (even when they continue to circulate the printed word) could be said to constitute a difference – a particular **spectral** effect – regarding oppositions that depend on a certain idea of distance, such as the opposition of domestic and foreign, us and them, private and public, etc. One of the principal effects of teletechnology, then, is to make it seem that all space is public, virtual or 'international' – and this affects political ideas of the republic ('the public thing') as such, along with the concept of the nation state. In this way 'teletechnology' refers not simply to **writing** in general, but in particular to whatever 'in general assures and determines the *spacing* of public space, the very possibility of the *res republica* and the phenomenality of the political' (SoM, 51). This is not to say that 'the media' have taken control of public opinion. But it is to acknowledge that whatever 'public opinion' is taken to mean these days is inseparable from its teletechnological forms of representation and distribution.

'No one, it seems to me,' as Derrida put it a decade before Gulf War II, 'can *contest* the fact that a dogmatics is attempting to install its worldwide hegemony in paradoxical and suspect conditions' (ibid.). It is indeed a paradox that anyone would seek to turn liberal democracy into dogma, but the point is that no one could attempt to do so today without recourse to teletechnology. The politically interventionist point, as it were, may be that no one could hope to resist such dogma by choosing to avoid a **responsibility** to engage with the operations and effects of teletechnology, especially when it comes to questions of the political 'itself'. (See also ARTIFACTUALITY, DEMOCRACY, EVENT, MESSIANISM, NEW INTERNATIONAL, SUPPLEMENTARITY, TEXT, VIRTUALITY.)

**text**    In the broadest sense a text is something that has been made or constructed (a novel, a movie, a legal document, a book of philosophy, etc.), implying that there are other things in the world (**being**, **justice**, truth and so on) which haven't been made but just are. According to this standard (**metaphysical**) view, we might say that everything in the world belongs either on the side of representation (text) or **presence** (the real).

Now when Derrida speaks of text he does so in the standard sense, but with a twist. Derrida's 'text' carries the sense of something that has been made – and that's all. In other words it doesn't carry the inference that, 'outside' the text, things just are. This has two consequences: first, that everything is text and so 'there is no outside-text' (OG, 158). Secondly, because everything is text, because there is nothing that is prior to textuality, then really there is no such thing as representation. A text is not, for Derrida, the imitation of a presence; instead presence is an effect of textuality. It does not follow from this that **deconstruction** is committed to understanding economic, political and historical forces (say) as 'fictional', or to regarding them as operating on the same plane as rhetorical devices. It does not mean that deconstruction is prevented from referring to **intentionality** or from having anything to say about **democracy**. 'What I call "text"', Derrida explains, 'implies all the **structures** called "real," "economic," "historical," socio-institutional, in short: all possible referents' (LI, 148). While these referents have their singularities (a camera angle is not the same as a shift in the economy), nonetheless they are not in themselves 'outside the text': at the very least the values and meanings that might be attributed to them are open to interpretation, according to the many possible contexts in which those interpretations could be made.

Again, though, what might be called the infinite (or indefinite) referentiality of the Derridean text should not be mistaken for a form of representation. What semiotics calls a referent is, for deconstruction, another text. 'That does not mean', Derrida writes, 'that all referents are suspended, denied, or enclosed in a book, as people have claimed, or have been naive enough to believe and to have accused me of believing'. What it means rather is that 'every referent, all reality has the structure of a differential **trace**, and that one cannot refer to this "real" except in an interpretive experience. The latter neither yields meaning nor assumes it except in a movement of differential referring. That's all' (LI, 148). So the claim that there is nothing outside of the text is an acknowledgment simply that you could never get to a point where something no longer referred to something else: there is nothing outside of context, that is to say. If you looked up the word 'cat' in a (**proper**) dictionary, for example, you would find its definition is comprised of words that are themselves the subject of dictionary definitions, and so on. As with every other word, the definition of 'cat' cannot stand on its own; its meaning is an effect of its differential relations within a system of referents. There is nothing outside this 'system'. Yes of course there are cats in the world, but there are no cats in the dictionary. And any reference to what we can call 'real' cats is still going to be a reference. You cannot get away from this by thinking that, from now on, instead of using the word 'cat' you're going to carry around a real cat with you wherever you go, so that when you need to refer to the animal that says 'meow' you can hold up the very thing-in-itself. Your real cat would still be a referent – and of course it would also, in a sense, be real. But its 'reality' would not be something that could exist outside of claims to know that it exists. Reality, in a word, is something that textuality posits. That's all. (See also ARTIFACTUALITY, DIFFERANCE, INSIDE–OUTSIDE, ITERABILITY, SPEECH–WRITING OPPOSITION, SUPPLEMENTARITY, UNDECIDABILITY, VIRTUALITY.)

**trace**   The dyadic **structure** of the sign constitutes it as a unity, the unity of the sensible and the intelligible, signifier and signified. Despite **Saussure**'s insistence on the arbitrariness of this structure, the sign remains (for him, as for the promised science of signs in general) the irreducible unit of signification. In this way semiotics is **logocentric**. For what the sign's unity occludes, on Derrida's account, is the necessity of its relations to an exteriority, to what is 'outside' the sign but nonetheless indissociable from it. Perhaps then we might refer to the sign as a unit-without-unity (see Lucy, *Beyond*). Or perhaps we need some new concepts to explain how meaning works. One of these (belonging to a sort of series that includes **differance, writing, supplement, text,** etc.) Derrida gives as the *trace* (or sometimes arche-trace), which functions to unsettle the sign's **metaphysical** determination.

Every system of signs is based on the **play** of differences within that system. This was Saussure's own recognition, the principle by which signification occurs. What the principle forbids is the possibility that 'a simple element be *present* in and of itself, referring only to itself' (P, 26). It forbids this from happening 'at any moment, or in any sense' (ibid.). From the very outset, then, the sign's 'unity', the stability of its 'dyadic' structure, is troubled by the principle of the play of differences as the ground of signification. According to this principle, as Derrida puts it, 'no element can function as a sign without referring to another element which itself is not simply present' (ibid.). All the 'elements' of a system are interwoven or inter-textualized together, each 'being constituted on the basis of the trace within it of the other elements of the chain or system' (ibid.). *On the basis of the trace*: there is something, then, that comes 'before' the sign. *The trace within it*: there is something, then, that remains 'after' the sign is constituted, which both effects that constitution and is inseparable from it.

This residue which both remains and comes before has a very strange ontology. Derrida's point, however, is that the quasi-ontology of the trace lends ontology to the sign. The ontological unity of the sign is an effect of the quasi-ontological non-presence of the trace, a non-presence that cannot be conceived of according to the opposition presence–absence. Hence the trace (or the arche-trace) is anterior even to Saussure's principle of the play of differences (or the quasi-transcendental condition by which a principle could appear as such): the trace is the **origin** of difference, 'the opening of the first exteriority in general, the enigmatic relationship of the living to its other and of an **inside** to an **outside**' (OG, 70). At the same time, in its quasi-anterior, quasi-ontological non-presence, the trace threatens the very idea of originality; it is the origin as non-origin, the origin effaced. In this it undermines presence and **identity**. 'The trace is not only the disappearance of origin – within the discourse that we sustain and according to the path that we follow it means that the origin did not even disappear, that it was never constituted except reciprocally by a nonorigin, the trace, which thus becomes the origin of the origin' (OG, 61). Like the supplement, the ***pharmakon***, differance and many other Derridean concepts, or what he sometimes refers to as an 'aconceptual concept' (LI, 118), the trace cannot be understood – it makes no sense – according to a standard logic of conceptual production by which every concept 'implies the alternative of "all or nothing"' (ibid.). Every concept must obey this rule, for what would a 'concept' be that was all and nothing at the same time, or neither all nor nothing? Like the supplement, the *pharmakon* and so on, the trace is unable to be thought within metaphysics. 'No ontology can think its operation', as Derrida remarks of the supplement, a concept, like that of the trace, which is not a concept strictly speaking or in any philosophically rigorous sense, since the supplement (again, like the trace) is 'neither a presence nor an absence' (OG, 314).

This is not to say that Derrida's non-concepts are all of a piece. 'They share a certain functional analogy', he notes, 'but remain singular and irreducible to one another, as are the textual chains from which they are inseparable' (LI, 155). Whatever is used to justify a concept can 'therefore never be absolute and definitive. It [the justification] corresponds to a condition of forces and translates an historical calculation' (OG, 70). Concepts have contexts, in other words; they 'receive meaning only in sequences of differences' (ibid.) that correspond to particular conditions and configurations. It is one of the structural deficiencies of a book such as this, a 'dictionary' of Derridean terms or concepts, that it can't quite situate the terms or concepts it 'defines' in the contexts from which they emerged and, from what Derrida says above, remain inseparable. There isn't the time or space, in other words, to 'contextualize' every entry in this book, although I'm well aware that in discussing these concepts 'out of context' there is a strong risk of them being seen either as 'interchangeable' with one another or of being taken for a set of 'tools' that can be 'applied' willy-nilly, without having to bother with what Derrida has to say about, say, the trace, over a number of texts or 'textual chains' and contexts. It goes without saying that Derrida has a lot more to say about the trace, and a good deal else, than I can say here; and of course it goes without saying too that it is not only the constraints of time and space that limit what I'm able to say on the question of what Derrida means by the trace, or indeed almost anything else.

All the same, Derrida explains that at least part of the justification for turning his attention to the trace comes from the importance given to this concept in Levinas's work on ethics (OG, 70). For Levinas, the primary ethical relationship is constituted in the turning of one face to another (see *Totality*). This 'original face-to-face', as Derrida argues in the essay 'Violence and Metaphysics', amounts to 'the emergence of absolute alterity, the emergence of an exteriority which can be neither derived, nor engendered, nor constituted on the basis of anything other than itself. An absolute outside, an exteriority infinitely overflowing the monad of the *ego cogito*' (WD, 106). The problem here is with the absoluteness, the infinity, that this conception of exteriority requires. Such radical exteriority accords a reassuring self-presence to the otherness of the other, to the point where others might as well be rocks or trees. But for Derrida the relation of an other to the self could never be explained as the difference between two presences, even if the other's 'presence' were to be attributed with a kind of primordial unknowability, perhaps as a mark of respect. The other as wholly other would be present to itself, an idea that would help to affirm the presence of selfhood – which could lead as easily to violence as to understanding. To approach others in terms of their non-exteriority, however, might lead to a conception of self–other relations based on traces of mutual implication and obligation rather than on structures of absolute difference. (See also BEING, INSIDE–OUTSIDE, ITERABILITY, RESPONSIBILITY, SPECTRALITY, SPEECH–WRITING OPPOSITION, YES.)

**undecidability**  Every decision is the result of a process. However right and natural it might appear, and even if it seems to take only a split second, each decision undergoes a struggle before it is made. Once made, every decision could always have been otherwise. It is in this sense that decisions are always undecidable, which is not to say either that there are no grounds for making decisions (so any decision will do: thumbs up, thumbs down – same difference) or that there isn't a pressing need for decisions to be made (speak out against injustice now, or later – it's all the same). Decisions are undecidable in so far as they are structured by the law of undecidability. While this is true of all decisions, Derrida's interest lies especially in decisions involving 'ethico-political **responsibility**' (LI, 116). Undecidability, then, is the 'necessary condition' of decidability (ibid.), but this is not really a problem when it comes to choosing whether to wear black or paisley. It's a problem primarily (it would be tempting, but wrong, to say 'only') when *responsibility* looms as a question – and yes of course there are times when the question of responsibility pertains to matters of style. So undecidability appears as a problem when, for example, it comes to choosing whether to vote left or right, to speak out against injustice now or later, or to defend a welfare system in spite of knowing that every system is open to exploitation. But even in some imagined space outside all consideration of ethics and politics, undecidability remains a problem for attempts to calculate the difference between (say) **structure** and **event** or *langue* and *parole* (see **Saussure**). In this – by raising questions for philosophy in the widest sense, as well as for ethics and politics – undecidability constitutes a general problem for **metaphysics**, operating at every level of decision-making and thought.

Ideally, every decision aspires to the status of a foregone conclusion, as though nothing had ever to be decided or as if every decision were somehow entirely 'self-made'. Law courts, for instance, don't make life-or-death decisions supposing that they might be wrong, sentencing this one to death row and letting that one go free according to chance. By weighing up all the evidence scrupulously, following procedures diligently, giving due regard to both sides and paying attention to every last detail (as it were) – chance is precisely what the court seeks ideally to eradicate, and in practice certainly to minimize. If court decisions were not taken to be irrefutable (despite often turning out to be wrong), courts would have no authority. If fortunes in a courtroom turned out to be as arbitrary, fluctuating, unpredictable, incalculable and frustrating as fortunes in a casino, what price **justice**?

The implication here is that, once made, every courtroom decision takes on the appearance of a foregone conclusion, each decision becoming the only one (despite the prevalence of appeals processes and what this says about the court's power to deliver infallible justice – and what would a court be that promised anything less?). This implication is no doubt reassuring, but that doesn't make it true. In fact, the difference between the courtroom and the gaming room is undecidable. Chance and calculability inhere in both, to varying degrees, on different days and nights, according to your luck.

To be sure, courts and casinos must conform to rules, or laws. But there are laws, and there are people. Sometimes rules are bent, or broken. On this day, money talks; on another, someone is tired or forgetful. Courts and casinos are not the same, but in what precise – irrefutable, transcendental, absolute, decontextualized, uncontroversial – ways are they different?

What would decide the difference, once and for all? And what would a difference be that remained undecided and therefore, perhaps, undecidable? Or to put this differently, what would a decidable difference be? This is not a question about differences between elements in the periodic table; it concerns differences within culture, involving judgement. What might count as a ground for judging whether this or that event constitutes a criminal act?

Derrida has no answer to this. There are those who say that therefore his 'philosophy' is apolitical, or at best that it's politically ineffective. The accusation harbours countless problems, but the fundamental one is that the difference between politics and indifference (or ineffectivity) is, first of all, calculable and secondly that it has to do with the **presence** or absence of something like a programme, an agenda, a position formed in advance of actual events which enables decisions to be taken as to whether those events should be supported or resisted. If you've got one of these programmes, you're political; if you don't, you're not.

What this means, however, is that the generality of any programme (system, structure, agenda, etc.) must overlook (or override) the singularity of any event, in all its complexity, its lived experience, its actuality. Whatever makes an event (**text**, **identity**, etc.) what 'it is' – constituting its irreducible singularity – is precisely what every programme or system must fail to countenance, engage with, respond to. *This* event, here and now (not anywhere else at another time) cannot remain what it is *and* be something else, the calculable outcome of a system of events. If the general structure of a programme were allowed to override the complex singularity of every ungeneralizable event (which is to say of every event in all its ungeneralizable singularity), there could be no such thing as culture or human history. If programmes could make decisions (of the responsible, Derridean variety), computers would be magistrates. If decisions were entirely calculable, they wouldn't be decisions. For something to be a decision, it has to risk being wrong. This is why Derrida says that every decision, in order to be a decision, has to pass through what he calls the '*experience and experiment of the undecidable*' (LI, 116). In order to be made, every decision (in this responsible, Derridean sense) has to be unprogrammable. A programmed decision would be no decision at all. A poet, for example, who set out to write a Shakespearean sonnet would not *decide* to conform to a certain metre and rhyme scheme, but we could never say that magistrates are bound in this way to laws (or to the law in general) such that a decision to execute, or not to execute, a prisoner would be of the same order as 'deciding' to end a Shakespearean sonnet with a couplet.

If an armed intruder were to break into Derrida's house one night, it would be preposterous to suppose that Derrida would say, 'Is that a text in your hand?'. Why suppose (as certain detractors must) that the Derrida whom we can reasonably believe knows that sometimes a gun is just a gun, is a different Derrida from the one who argues that differences are undecidable? Like everyone else, Derrida makes decisions all the time. Undecidability should not, in other words, be mistaken for some kind of paralysis when it comes to having to make moral and political decisions, let alone other types. It is instead the condition on which any decision (especially those concerning ethico-political responsibility) comes to pass.

For a decision to be other than programmed – for it to be a decision in this Derridean sense – it must exceed or overrun the conditions of any programme. If it's to be made by an ethical being, rather than a computer, a decision must be allowed to pass through a struggle – Derrida calls it a 'trial' (LI, 116) or an 'ordeal' (FoL, 24) – within the time and space of which it cannot be known what the eventual outcome will be, because at least more than one possibility remains open. A decision that could not have been otherwise would not be a decision.

But once a decision has been made, undecidability doesn't simply stop. That is not by a long stretch where the matter ends. The relationship between a decision and undecidability is not of the order of a scoreline, as though the point were to defeat or overcome undecidability (decision 1, undecidability 0). If this were so, a decision would become a foregone conclusion; it would be as if the decision were absolutely and irrefutably right in advance, in which case no responsibility – no risk – would be entailed in making it. Every decision must engage afresh, for another first time, with the singularity of the occasion that calls for a decision to be made. Every judgement must be a new judgement, a new 'experience and experiment of the undecidable', but this is not to say that judgements should be made intuitively or by free association, disregarding all laws and conventions, routine practices, normative procedures and the like. A judgement that had no back-up, which was entirely unsupported by any reference whatsoever to rules and procedures of any kind, would lack all authority or effectivity. Undecidability is not therefore a ruse for avoiding the force of law or, worse, the force of structure, as if **deconstruction** held to the completely ridiculous notion that structures don't exist.

Again, though, if decisions were simply effects of structures (programmes, laws, etc.) they wouldn't be decisions. This is why deconstruction sides with undecidability, without being against decisions or rendering itself incapable of making them. It is also why undecidability never stops; 'the ordeal of undecidability' does not reach a limit, come to an end or get overcome, when a decision is made, which is why Derrida sometimes refers to 'the **ghost** of the undecidable' (FoL, 24) as that which haunts every decision, preventing it from coming to **presence** or being seen as self-authorized and inviolable, as though it could never have been otherwise. Indeed, in principle, this very ghost-like quality of the condition of its always being possible for a decision to have been otherwise, keeps decisions from becoming the basis for new laws, new programmes, new attitudes by which to make decisions in the future. In practice, of course, 'the ghost of the undecidable' is routinely ignored (and along with it the sense of deep responsibility involved in decision-making), such that national immigration policies, say, are never 'racist' or 'imperialist' but only ever 'protectionist', designed to defend an idea of cultural identity against contamination by the other whose every singular call is generalized as the illegitimate demand for a handout, a free ride, a chance to get something for nothing.

Undecidability opens every decision (and keeps it open) to the possibility of being otherwise. The key point is that undecidability does not refer to the difficulty of sometimes having to decide between competing choices, or to 'the oscillation between two significations or two contradictory and very determinate rules, each equally imperative' (FoL, 24). We may experience some (even much) difficulty in deciding which shirt to wear on a given day, but this wouldn't count as an ordeal requiring us to take responsibility for what remains 'obliged – it is of obligation that we must speak – to give itself up to the impossible decision, while taking account of law and rules' (ibid.). Nevertheless it should be recognized that something like a 'lower-order' or quasi-formal undecidability operates within the structure of any binary opposition, so that the terms of any binary pair (signifier–signified, **speech–writing** and so on) are held in a relation of non-absolute, incomplete, non-oppositional difference. In a word they are caught in relations not of difference, but **differance**. If undecidability (or indeed differance, **supplementarity**, the *pharmakon*, etc.) were taken to mean only this 'quasi-formal' condition, then the charge that deconstruction is obscurantist, politically evasive, socially uncommitted and the like would weigh very heavily. In response it should be noted not that differance is the 'formalist' or 'apolitical' version of undecidability, but rather that what might be called the project of deconstruction can be construed as an ongoing encounter with 'the ordeal of the undecidable'. This would be to say that deconstruction is always a deconstruction *of* something – something which can be put here as particular instances of concepts that seem to be undeconstructible, such as *identity, self-presence* and *authority*. For deconstruction to matter, the positivity of these concepts would need to be seen to depend on an irresponsible refusal to confront 'the ghost of the undecidable'. (See also APORIA, DISSEMINATION, GIFT, KANT, POSTAL METAPHOR, SPECTRALITY, WRITING, YES.)

**virtuality**   In the first *Toy Story* movie (1995), Buzz Lightyear believes that he is actually a space ranger and not a toy, a child's plaything. This brilliantly simple conceit – a variation on the narrator's misunderstanding of herself as himself in Iain Banks's *The Wasp Factory* (1984) – generates most of the gags and much of the action for the majority of the film. We know of course from the outset that Buzz is not who he thinks he is, and so we can see that his delusion proves that there really isn't any difference, as Derrida puts it (in another context), between 'being sure' and 'wanting to be sure' (SoM, 38). We don't discover this until near the end of *The Wasp Factory*, but that is neither here nor there for now.

Although Buzz has a very different experience of actuality from the other characters in *Toy Story* (and from us), nonetheless he thinks and acts (as do the other toys and as we do) on the basis of an absolute distinction between what is and is not actual. Everyone else knows that the world in which Buzz operates is a *virtual* world, but that doesn't stop things from happening – on the contrary. We know that Buzz does not belong to an intergalactic alliance of good guys opposed to the imperial forces of the Evil Emperor Zurg, but the fact that he believes he does is what produces many actions and events in the film's representation of the *actual* world. (All of this is true as well in *The Wasp Factory*, although we can't know that until we get to the revelation of the narrator's 'sex change' at the end.)

What *Toy Story* serves to show, then, is that the difference between 'virtual' reality and 'actual' reality is not quite as assured as we might want it to be. Let's concede, for example, that there is no such person as the Evil Emperor Zurg – he's just a projection of Buzz Lightyear's deluded version of reality. Now it turns out in *Toy Story 2* (1999) that Zurg does in fact exist, albeit not as a person but as a toy. And the joke here is that Zurg turns out to be exactly what Buzz said he was in the first film – an evil emperor from another planet. Or really the joke is that he thinks he's an evil emperor from another planet – in fact he's just another deluded toy, like Buzz in the first film and the other Buzz Lightyears in the sequel.

But let's go back to the original concession: there *is* no Evil Emperor Zurg. The most that could be said is that Zurg's 'existence' is entirely virtual. We posit his existence, but we know that he does not actually exist as such. Even when he appears in the second film we know that he is not the Evil Emperor Zurg from another planet – he's a toy. So everything that is used to construct the actuality of Zurg's existence is in fact virtual – he exists only because Buzz says he exists, in the first place, and thereafter only because Zurg 'himself' says that he actually is an evil emperor from another planet and behaves accordingly. Again, everything about Zurg's actuality is virtual – constructed (made up) out of signs, representations, simulacra. But to say that his actuality is virtual is not to say, clearly, that it isn't actual; it's to say that his actual virtuality – or 'actuvirtuality', as Derrida sometimes calls it – is constituted outside the ontological opposition of the actual and the virtual.

This is true, Derrida argues, of actuality in general, especially as constructed by **teletechnology** today. What counts as actuality now, in other words, necessitates 'a concept of *virtuality* (virtual image, virtual space, and so virtual **event**) that can doubtless no longer be opposed, in perfect philosophical serenity, to actual reality in the way that philosophers used to distinguish between power and act, *dynamis* and *energia*' and so forth (EoT, 6). Take 'the Middle East' or 'Islam', for example. Both of these **spectres** (or these twin guises of the one spectre) exert considerable actuality today, but do so in a way that demonstrates what Derrida means by actuality having to include an aspect of virtuality, in the form say of virtual space. For the actuality of 'the Middle East' or 'Islam' cannot be accounted for simply by referring to an actual place on a map, or by reference to their (or its) location in time understood simply as history. Hence to allude to the virtual space – or *the virtual reality* – of 'the Middle East' is not at all to avoid being political; it is on the contrary (and among things) to politicize what is at stake in the avoidance of trying to analyse the ways and means by which the actuality of 'the Middle East' or 'Islam' has been and continues to be made. The always necessarily virtual dimension of actuality 'affects both the time and the space of the image, of discourse, of "information," in short, everything that refers us to this so-called actuality, to the implacable reality of its supposed present' (EoT, 6). In trying to get us to think about the virtuality of the actual, however, Derrida is not suggesting that today's reality is some kind of postmodern illusion of the real, an effect of everyone spending too much time on the Internet and watching too much television. Yet certainly we could say that the project of **deconstruction** is directed against a way of thinking that 'smells of clean linen', as a character in one of Sartre's novels (almost) puts it (*Age*, 13), or against a **metaphysics** of tidy distinctions between this ontological category (such as the actual) and that one (the virtual), the acceptance of which goes hand in hand with the avoidance of **responsibility**.

Simply to accept that actuality has nothing to do with virtuality, or to think that the actual is what happens and the virtual is always what is made (even if only by an act of the imagination), would be to avoid taking responsibility for not seeing many real-historical events in the world today *as* events, because they don't conform to the concept of an event understood in terms of the opposition of the actual and the virtual. Events are not reducible to what appear only as news items on television. While actuality is always produced, it is not produced only by 'the media' – and never in the sense of being purely fabricated (but see **hymen**). It is precisely because actuality is always produced that we have a responsibility to analyse its production and a responsibility to produce actuality ourselves – to make our own **texts** or artefacts out of what is going on in the world today. For example: unemployment. 'The function of social inactivity', as Derrida puts it, 'of non-work or of underemployment is entering into a new era. It calls for another politics. And another concept' (SoM, 81). This 'new' unemployment – 'that more or less well-calculated deregulation of a new market, new technologies, new worldwide competitiveness' (ibid.) – doesn't feature in the news, because it doesn't count as an event according to the opposition of the actual and the virtual. It doesn't occupy a certain place and time, even though it's undeniably with us here and now. Without question, Derrida (although not only him) has produced its actuality, but not in such a way that his description of the new unemployment could be dismissed as a figment of the imagination.

Likewise, we could say that the *production* of Osama bin Laden today provides a timely instance of a real-life equivalent of the actuvirtuality of the Evil Emperor Zurg. This would not be to say (as should be clear by now) that Osama bin Laden isn't real, but rather that whatever we might take his actuality to be (or the actuality of a 'global terrorist network') cannot be separated into a neat and tidy distinction from an understanding of the virtual. To continue to think of the actual in terms of **presence** (which is how actuality is conceptualized on television, for example), and not in terms of its relations to the virtual, would be to go on thinking in a way that 'smells of clean linen'. And that's the way Buzz Lightyear thinks. The concept of virtuality (or actuvirtuality) calls for a different way of thinking, a way of thinking **differance**. (See also ARTIFACTUALITY, IDENTITY, UNDECIDABILITY, WRITING.)

**writing**    As I start out to write this sentence I am not absolutely sure how it will end. The only way I could have known exactly where I was going with that sentence (or any sentence) would be if I had a crystal ball, if somehow I could see into the future. Since I don't believe in clairvoyance, I don't believe anyone can see what hasn't happened yet. And every time anyone sits down to write a sentence (or to compose one mentally), the end remains to come; whatever 'happens' happens later, even if the interval between the beginning and the end lasts only for a split second.

Now of course sentences are governed by grammatical rules. With every sentence there is always a relation between the beginning and the end – you can't just end a sentence any which way you goobledegook. But these rules are never so constraining that the beginning *determines* the ending. There is always the element of surprise to be reckoned with – the chance that a sentence might end in a way you couldn't have predicted when you started writing it, or started reading it.

Whether we look at writing from the point of view of writers or readers, then, one of the defining features of writing seems to be that its effects are never quite controllable. To write or to read is to be in a position of openness to the possibility of unexpected or chance effects. This possibility is exploited in literature, but it also conditions writing generally. Whatever ends up being written (a poem, a news story, a government report, etc.) is always at some remove from its referent, from the so-called thing itself (in the form of a feeling, a real-historical **event**, a socio-political situation, etc.) that could be said to have occasioned the writing. The necessity of this gap between writing and reality (let's say) is seen as cause for both celebration and consternation: it's a good thing as far as literature goes, leading to all manner of rhetorical and stylistic possibilities that can open onto imaginative avenues for thinking differently about reality, but it's potentially a bad thing in just about all other respects because it can lead to misrepresentations and misunderstandings of reality's 'true nature'. So the gap between writing and reality is something to be exploited for imaginative purposes but is otherwise a danger or a problem that has to be overcome for any kind of writing (such as philosophical writing) that purports to 'contain' a prior truth. It's fine then for John Donne to compare (in the poem 'A Valediction: Forbidding Mourning', written in the early seventeenth century) the relationship between two lovers to the twin arms of a compass, such that even when the lovers are apart their love draws them together within a circle, but there are very few other contexts in which that conceit could appear as anything other than inappropriately florid, potentially misleading or 'ungrammatical'.

In what is called literature, we might say that writing draws attention to itself at the level of the signifier. We might say in turn that writing as literature has appropriated or been allowed to own this attention to the signifier as its special property or **proper** object, the better that other forms of writing may define themselves against such attention. Certainly in the case of philosophical writing, an attention to the signifier is not a priority. On the contrary, the basic rule of philosophical writing is to make the signifier as transparent as possible, its only function being to focus attention on the signified (albeit **Nietzsche** is a notable exception here). But as Derrida points out consistently, the distinction between literature and other kinds of writing serves a sort of dream – the dream of what might be called the possibility of a form of writing that operates at the level of 'degree zero' representation. The more it is allowed, in other words, that literature owns the signifier, the more it can seem that philosophy (say) knows a different way of writing, a way of closing the gap between writing and reality (or **presence**). Since in fact it is impossible to close that gap, philosophy can be written only in such a way as to distance itself from literature in the hope of being seen to distance itself from writing. In a word, philosophy suppresses everything in writing that literature exploits.

What this seems to set up is something like a distinction between the literary and the literal, but note that what sets it up is philosophy's *suppression* of everything associated with the kind of writing that is seen to specialize in drawing attention to the signifier – in drawing attention to itself *as* writing. Yet while writing is understood traditionally in terms of absence (the absence of the referent and the absence of the one who writes), the defining absences of writing do not extend to the absence of the signifier. The persistence of the signifier in writing, and as writing, is something that neither philosophy nor any kind of writing could hope to 'overcome'. Hence the persistence of the signifier in writing (and as writing) is not exterior to philosophy but is rather always within philosophy itself, dividing philosophy *from* 'itself' as the absolute other of writing. This doesn't mean that philosophy has no **identity**; it means that it does not have an identity defined in terms of an absolute **inside–outside** separation. Indeed it is precisely the non-oppositional or non-absolute nature of that separation – or that difference – which makes it possible for philosophy to have an identity at all. Philosophy's identity depends on its non-identity to – or difference from – its other in the form of writing. Its identity depends on difference.

From this it can be said that a general difference precedes the formation of every particular difference, and the name Derrida gives to this general difference is *writing* (though he also uses other names such as **differance, dissemination, supplementarity** and **trace**). Where does the distinction between philosophy and literature come from? It comes from (or is held within) the **structure** of an opposition: the identity or self-sufficiency of philosophy *depends* on its difference from literature, and vice versa. The necessity of this difference – of this dependence on the other – contradicts the notion that philosophy or literature is 'self-sufficient', or the idea that each is grounded in presence. The lack of presence in philosophy and literature opens each of them to the other. So this 'lack' functions as a passage or avenue of exchange pointing in two directions at once: outside-in and inside-out. Such is the openness, the fluidity, the ungroundedness, the indeterminacy that has always been associated with writing as a system of representation.

As Derrida argues in his discussion of the **speech–writing opposition**, writing has always been understood as a technology for copying speech. Neither the writer nor the referent is ever 'in' writing, and these two absences characterize the structure of the written **mark** or sign. But Derrida's argument is that the non-presence associated with writing conditions the very possibility of all signs, regardless of their technological forms. There is no such thing as a non-technological or non-grammatological sign.

Consider the structure of the so-called written sign. It consists of a general spacing: the space between letters makes it possible to form words, the space between words makes it possible to form sentences and so on.

So these spaces are in fact productive or generative – they constitute the work of spacing. And this work is spatio-temporal: the distribution of written marks occurs not only across a page or screen, but also across time. A sentence, for example, unfolds spatio-temporally. Its ending differs from its beginning, and its completion depends on its ending having to be held back or deferred from arriving too soon. Without this differing and deferring, no sentence could signify. But neither could any written sign. For the written word 'at' to be recognized as a sign, 't' has to follow 'a' in space and come after it in time. But 'a' and 't' also have to differ from one another, while the *word* 'at' has to be deferred from arriving as a word or sign until 't' comes after 'a'. And of course it doesn't stop there. For 'at' to signify as an English word, it has to differ from other words and so it can never arrive at being a word on its own – its 'completion' or 'self-constitution' is endlessly deferred.

Derrida could be said to ask a simple question of all this: what's so special about the written sign? Differing and deferring, the work of spacing, absence of presence – these all belong to the structure of the sign in general. They are not restricted to the written sign. Hence the so-called special features of the written sign comprise a set of general conditions by which every sign (spoken, written, visual, etc.) is constituted. Or rather in a sense these general conditions, since they lead to the production of nothing permanent, undermine the very notion of the sign's constitution, the idea of an 'entity' or a 'unit' being constituted in the relationship of signifier to signified. Because the signified is never 'outside' the sign, every so-called signified is always in fact another signifier. The signifier–signified relationship, then, is never one simply of conjunction or constitution; there is always an effect of disjunction or interruption at work in any signifier's movement towards a signified. Again this has nothing to do exclusively with written signs but is true of all signs generally. Every 'sign' is the trace of an absent referent, and there could never be any teleological, temporal or spatial 'end' to the **play** and movement of differential traces that belongs to the idea of writing in the narrow sense but which (on Derrida's account) must come before the separation of writing-as-representation and speech-as-presence.

Derrida's 'writing' refers therefore to the general spatio-temporal distribution of marks (spacing in general) that is the quasi-transcendental condition by which non-spoken signs are understood as 'representational'. One of the purposes of making us think about general writing or spacing is to move us away from notions of representation, which always infer the presence and priority of the thing that is re-presented. Similarly, the notion of signification imputes a certain presence and priority to signifieds and referents, despite **Saussure**'s assertions to the contrary. Because the structure of the inscriptive mark or 'gram' is typical of signs in general, then, Derrida argues that all meaning-effects are products of a general system of differences which is *grammatological* rather than 'semiotic' or 'representational' in nature. In this way all signs belong to a general order of grammatology, such that no sign is purely non-grammatological or non-inscriptive. So even visual signs, for example, are 'writerly'. As Derrida put it not so long ago at one of the Sydney seminars, 'what one calls visual art is a form of writing which is neither subjected in a hierarchical manner to verbal discourse nor to the claim of authority that **logocentric** philosophy would like to confirm over the visual arts' (DE, 22–3). The visual is writerly because, that is to say, it is 'never totally "pure," never free of traces' (DE, 23). All drives to purity can proceed only from a failure to acknowledge what drives them.

> What drives them is a spacing, a *khora* that prevents them from reaching their purity. This obstacle, this limit to the pure and full plenitude and fulfillment of this drive (be it optical, haptic or musical), is not a negative failure nor is it a threat. It is also a chance, an opening of the desire of the drive. This obstacle is the condition of possibility of the drive itself. (ibid.)

What is an *obstacle* that offers both 'a chance' and 'an opening'? Such a question might be said to define without defining what Derrida means by 'writing'. As understood by **metaphysics**, writing *obstructs* the fulfilment of purity and presence (thought as presence, **being** as presence and so on), but on Derrida's account it is the very condition by which purity and presence are able to exert any power or authority at all. Purity and presence are grammatological effects, effects of a general writing. There is nothing outside this general writing and inside it nothing that is pure and full of presence. (See also ARTIFACTUALITY, ITERABILITY, PHONOCENTRISM, POSTAL METAPHOR, TELETECHNOLOGY, TEXT.)

**yes** 'I promise' – these are the last words of New York writer Paul Auster's grim little tale of city life in ruins, *In the Country of Last Things* (1987). Written in epistolary form (as a kind of secular retelling of the biblical book of Revelation), the book could be said to reflect on the following question: what might be left when everything seems to be gone? What could turn out to be the very last thing of all? No doubt the tone of such a question is apocalyptic, and no doubt Auster's story is a dystopia. But, like every **text**, this little novel does not quite belong to any genre: it is neither simply epistolary nor simply dystopic. It doesn't help to call it a novel, either. And despite its undeniably apocalyptic tone the book leaves us with nothing quite so grand as a revelation – a vision of what the present will become in the future unless we start to fix things now. All these generic expectations, as it were, lead us up the garden path (as generic expectations are often wont to do). For in the end what is left, all that is left, is not a dystopic feeling of nothingness, not an apocalyptic revelation, not a unifying moral, but just these few inconclusive words: 'I will try to write to you again, I promise.'

This is not so much an ending as simply where the novel stops. But it is also, in a sense, where the novel begins, where everything begins – with a promise. To make a promise is to say 'yes', to make an affirmation – *yes, I promise* (to tell you a story, to love you for ever, to quit smoking, etc.) – constituting a kind of opening to the future. A promise always marks an inauguration: in the act of promising, one promises to inaugurate a process that will lead to the fulfilment of one's promise in a time to come. But that's not a guarantee, albeit some promises are easier to keep than others. I could promise to wear a pair of sunglasses tomorrow that resemble as closely as possible the pair that Peter Fonda wears in *Easy Rider* (1969), for example, and have reason to believe that I may be able to keep my promise. But I could not say to my son, 'Yes, I promise to love you and look after you for as long as I live', and expect to have done with it. You can't say 'yes' to **responsibility** and leave it at that. After saying 'yes' to my son I would have to say (without necessarily having to say it) 'yes' again and again, over and over, each and every day, throughout all the days of my life. There would never come a time (when he was 18, for instance, or 21, or became a father himself) when I could say, to him or to me, that I have kept my promise and so now 'I now longer have to love you and look after you'. It doesn't work like that; no promise does. When you say 'yes' you always have to say 'yes' again. You could never say on your wedding day to the person you were marrying, 'Yes, for now'. Vows don't have use-by dates, even though we know that many marriages end in a broken promise: they don't conclude, they just stop (and not always for reasons that are explicable). To say 'yes' at your wedding – to say 'I do' – is to say what always has to be repeated, even (if needs be) after you're divorced (or at least this may be true for one of you, perhaps). What the originary 'yes' inaugurates, then, is a future that remains to come, which always includes the possibility of turning out otherwise than you might have imagined or desired. But for as long as you keep on saying 'yes' you will continue to honour the memory of the originary 'yes' – the wedding 'yes', as it were – and the future it inaugurates.

There is nothing prior to this inauguration; no one can be forced to say 'yes'. I could never say 'yes' to my son out of a sense of paternal obligation or because of any social pressure to feed, shelter and care for him. Class, gender, history, national spirit, cultural tradition – none of these is a condition of saying 'yes' to your child or the one you marry. To feel a duty or an obligation to say 'yes' would not be to say 'yes'. A 'yes' that was not unprecedented, which was not absolutely originary, would not be a 'yes'. Even so, while every 'yes' is originary, it always has to go on being said, it has to be repeated: its originariness does not fill it with **presence**. If when you say 'yes' for the first time you are being genuine, you have to keep on saying 'yes'. Every originary 'yes' is structured by **iterability**. 'You cannot say "yes"', as Derrida writes, 'without saying "yes, yes"' (VR, 27).

We might see here a sort of groundless ground of community. A genuine community, as it might be called, is founded on a promise; its **origin** is not (à la **Heidegger**) a gathering of **beings** united in their common spirit, or a grouping of those who participate in a cultural, political, religious or some other shared **identity**, but rather a simple promise to open and maintain a relation to others. Reduced to such a minimal condition the very concept of community no longer seems appropriate. When I say 'yes' to another, that is, I inaugurate a promise to remain open to whatever might come, to others who may come unexpectedly or in forms I may not have been able to predict. It is this, and not my nation's laws or my culture's traditions, that puts me in touch (very loosely) with a sense of 'community' – one which is not organized around a notion of identity but which is organized without being organized around differences (because difference is always plural). Certainly this could be said to be the theme of Auster's *In the Country of Last Things*, where the story that Anna Blume (the one who promises to write again) tells in her letter to the unnamed 'frame' narrator is that of a city reduced to a kind of primal state of disorder. No one knows how or why this happened; no one can say whether any official authority remains in charge. So everyone is driven only by a base need to survive, to go on living (though some choose not to), in the absence of anything that might be called a binding sense of community purpose or a shared historical project. Slowly, things start to disappear, people start to forget. But not even memory loss conforms to a common experience; not even what gets forgotten is able to supply, however sardonically, the basis of a 'gathering'. Anna writes:

> In the end, the problem is not so much that people forget, but that they do not always forget the same thing. What still exists as a memory for one person can be irretrievably lost for another, and this creates difficulties, insuperable barriers against understanding. How can you talk to someone about airplanes, for example, if that person doesn't know what an airplane is? It is a slow but ineluctable process of erasure. (Auster, *Last Things*, 88–9)

It gets worse, for after a while even language starts to disintegrate.

> Entire categories of objects disappear – flowerpots, for example, or cigarette filters, or rubber bands – and for a time you will be able to recognize those words, even if you cannot recall what they mean. But then, little by little, the words become only sounds, a random collection of glottals and fricatives, a storm of whirling phonemes, and finally the whole thing just collapses into gibberish. The word 'flowerpot' will make no more sense to you than the word 'slandigo.' Your mind will hear it, but it will register as something incomprehensible, a word from a language you cannot speak. (*Last Things*, 89)

But of course, because linguistic disintegration (or what Derrida might call **dissemination**) isn't uniform, then it is as if (both here and elsewhere, in a sense) 'each person is speaking his own private language, and as the instances of shared understanding diminish, it becomes increasingly difficult to communicate with anyone' (ibid.).

Maybe Auster's book is a fictive version of the French philosopher Jean-François Lyotard's argument (in *The Postmodern Condition*) that contemporary experience is defined by the loss of 'metanarratives' or totalizing beliefs. This might be another of its genres, albeit I'm not suggesting that Auster must have read Lyotard before he wrote *In the Country of Last Things*. But it does seem fair to say (although Auster never uses words like 'metanarrative' or 'postmodernism') that the novel is about what happens when a community loses any sense of participating in a shared experience, or when there's no one left who believes in 'grand stories' of historical progress, universal values, the triumph of **democracy** and the like. And what happens, perhaps, is that Anna Blume and the few others with whom she comes together at the end, find a way of conjoining which doesn't have (because it doesn't require) a **proper** name. In any case it couldn't be called a 'gathering' or a 'community', since these always invoke some sort of organizing principle (or metanarrative) concerning myths of national destiny, cultural vitality, political validation and the like. There is always, moreover, a sense in which communities seem to need to know where they're going, to know what the future will look like (which is impossible, of course) and a sense, too, in which every community is always a gathering of only some at the exclusion of others. This is not how Anna and her friends are held together, if anything 'holds' them together at all. If theirs is a 'community', it is one only in the loosest and most precarious sense. Yet by the same token, perhaps, it is also a community in a deep and originary sense – one based on the promise of remaining open to the future and the coming of others. Anna and her motley group of friends say 'yes' to one another; 'yes, yes' to the future-to-come. 'Everyone else is asleep', she writes, coming to an end which also opens the possibility of a new beginning,

> and I am sitting downstairs in the kitchen, trying to imagine what is ahead of me. I cannot imagine it. I cannot even begin to think of what will happen to us out there. Anything is possible, and that is almost the same as nothing, almost the same as being born into a world that has never existed before. . . .
> The only thing I ask for now is the chance to live one more day. This is

Anna Blume, your old friend from another world. Once we get to where we are going, I will try to write to you again, I promise. (*Last Things*, 187–8)

Of course, the most famous instance of a work of literature that ends on a promise is Joyce's *Ulysses*, whose last word is Molly's 'Yes', although Derrida notes (in 'Ulysses Gramophone') that 'yes' appears several hundred times in the novel. 'Yes' isn't just Molly's word; it's Joyce's too – his signature word, perhaps, if not his very signature as such or at least one of his signature effects. And like the word 'yes', every signature effects a promise. Every signature tries to consign the present to the future by saying, 'I was produced in a present that is now former and I will remain what I am in every present to come, as will the truth of everything I have been used to validate'. But the problem is that a promise is not a promise unless it is repeated, again and again. 'You cannot say "yes" without saying "yes, yes".' The further problem is that signatures are all too easy to forge.

By seeking to suppress the work of iterability, every signature tries to pass itself off in terms of a pure originality. It says 'yes' only once, as it were. But this (as we know) is not a sufficient condition for something to count as a promise. A promise is never a 'one-off'. There is always a first promise, an originary 'yes', but never one that is *original* in the sense of being full of plenitude and presence from the start, so that any repetition of it would be only possible but not necessary. To repeat an 'original' promise (if there is such a thing) would be simply to copy it, but not to confirm it again as if for another first time, as though each time you say 'yes' you are 'being born into a world that had never existed before'. If you want to make a promise that really is a promise, you have to keep on making it. All the force of your originary conviction demands that once you have said 'yes', you are committed to saying it again and again. Paradoxically, then, a truly false or fake promise would be one that tried to pass itself off as original.

It gets worse, however, because how could you tell that a promise you may make today, in all good faith, with every intention of keeping it, will be kept? How could you know that your promise *will* turn out to be an inauguration? Neither a promise in itself nor the depth of your conviction is any guarantee of what might happen in the future. When we make a promise, we promise an inauguration. 'But who knows?' Derrida asks. 'We will see' (VR, 27).

The difference between a 'genuine' and a 'false' promise, then, is **undecidable**. We could not even say that the repetition or the reaffirmation of a

promise proves that it must be genuine, since it is easy to repeat something mechanically, without any real conviction at all. Lots of people say
'I do' when really they mean 'I don't', for instance. So the mere repetition
of a promise or a 'yes' is not enough. 'You can say "yes, yes" like a parrot',
as Derrida points out. 'The technical reproduction of the originary "yes"
is from the beginning a threat to the living origin of the "yes." So the "yes"
is haunted by its own mechanical **ghost**, from the beginning. The second
"yes" will have to reinaugurate, to reinvent, the first one' (VR, 28). It's
here that Derrida sees a correlation between the **structure** of the 'yes' and
the structure of the signature, especially concerning Joyce. For if 'yes' is
one of Joyce's signature effects (a signature is not reducible to a proper
name, for Derrida; it marks something like the idiosyncratic or singular
'weave' of a **text** or a writer's 'style'), then the work of reinaugurating or
reinventing the 'yes' has to be carried out by others, through readings and
interpretations of Joyce's writing. Each of these readings, belonging to the
giddy enterprise of Joycean scholarship, acts as a 'countersignature'. But
it's not that Joyce's signature has to be countersigned by others now that
Joyce himself is dead and can't say 'yes' any more, since even when he was
alive his writing circulated in his absence. Rather, from the very start, his
signature could emerge as his alone only by way of passing through what
Tony Thwaites calls a 'detour' in the form of its relations with others
(other signatures, other ways of writing, other texts). His 'original' signature
will always have been a countersignature. 'Joyce's work will be incessantly
concerned with questions of the signature,' Thwaites argues, 'of author-
ization, claim, filiation, inheritance, right: not as things which are to be
defended against others, but as claims which the signature can make only
*in* this detour of and through the other' (*Temporalities*, 26). While this
may be true of the structure of the signature in general (every original
signature is an effect of an originary countersignature, we could say), what
interests Derrida about Joyce's signature in particular is that it seems to
anticipate everything it might be possible to say about it. It's as if his
signature incorporates every possible countersignature, as though in his
writing Joyce had found a way of incorporating the future. Is this his 'way'
of writing? Is *this* his signature? Is this its claim to be original?

This is a far cry from suggesting that Joyce's writing is undeconstructible
or full of presence. For although Derrida thinks it may be just about
impossible to say anything new about Joyce, something to which Joyce
himself hasn't said 'yes' already, this doesn't mean he thinks that Joyce's
writing is a finished product. It doesn't mean he thinks that Joyce 'himself'

– as an **intentional**, psychological **being** – once held in his own mind everything it could be possible to say about the styles, meanings, allusions, competencies and so forth that go to make up his work. It means rather that his *writing* – Joyce's signature – says 'yes' to everything. It doesn't need to be countersigned.

Hence, a paradox. On the one hand every signature aspires to be seen as the sign of an absolute presence, to be untranslatable, while on the other it always reaches out for confirmation, for the other's countersignature. As Derrida puts it, 'we must write, we must sign, we must bring about new events with untranslatable **marks** – and this is the frantic call, the distress of a signature that is asking for a *yes* from the other, the pleading injunction for a counter-signature' (UG, 283). In Joyce, however, 'the singular novelty of any other *yes*, of any other signature' has been anticipated (ibid.). So there's no choice but to say 'yes' to Joyce, meaning (in a sense) that he forces us to say 'yes'. But it's a kind of playful (or democratic) forcefulness, compared for instance to the coerciveness of the Bush administration in trying to get us to say 'yes' to the invasion of Iraq, which would result in turning it into the country of last things. Who would want to say 'yes' to that? Who'd want to stop there? (See also DIFFERANCE, HYMEN, INTENTIONALITY, MESSIANISM, NEW INTERNATIONAL, NIETZSCHE, POSTAL METAPHOR, SPECTRALITY, SUPPLEMENTARITY.)

# References

## Image

*Addams Family, The*. Dir. Barry Sonnenfeld. Paramount, 1991.

*Addams Family Values*. Dir. Barry Sonnenfeld. Paramount, 1993.

*Blair Witch Project, The*. Dir. Daniel Myrick and Eduardo Sanchez. Artisan, 1999.

*Breathless*. Dir. Jean-Luc Godard. Fox Lorber, 1961.

*Easy Rider*. Dir. Dennis Hopper. Columbia, 1969.

*Sweet Smell of Success, The*. Dir. Alexander Mackendrick. MGM/UA, 1957.

*Toy Story*. Dir. John Lasseter. Disney/Pixar, 1995.

*Toy Story 2*. Dir. Lee Unkrich. Disney/Pixar, 1999.

*Unforgiven*. Dir. Clint Eastwood. Warner, 1992.

*Witness for the Prosecution*. Dir. Billy Wilder. MGM/UA, 1957.

## Music

Brown, James. '(Get Up I Feel like Being a) Sex Machine', in *Godfather of Soul*. Karussell, 1993.

Dylan, Bob. 'Like a Rolling Stone', in *Highway 61 Revisited*. CBS, 1967.

Dylan, Bob. *Slow Train Coming*. Columbia, 1979.

Eminem, 'The Way I Am', in *The Marshall Mathers LP*. Interscope, 2000.

Funkadelic. 'One Nation under a Groove', in *Funk Gets Stronger*. Delta, 1999.

Halliwell, Geri. 'It's Raining Men', in *Scream if You Want to Go Faster*. EMI, 2001.

John, Elton. 'I Guess that's Why They Call It the Blues', in *Greatest Hits, 1976–1986*. Uptown/Universal, 2001.

Peaches, *The Teaches of Peaches*. Kitty-Yo, 2000.

Pop, Iggy. 'Nazi Girlfriend', in *Avenue B*. Virgin, 1999.

Ronettes, The. '(The Best Part of) Breakin' Up', in *The Best of the Ronettes*. ABKCO, 1992.

Triffids, The. 'The Seabirds', in *Born Sandy Devotional*. White, 1986.

Velvet Underground, The. 'I'm Waiting for the Man', in *The Velvet Underground & Nico*. MGM, 1967.

Weather Girls, The. 'It's Raining Men', in *Super Hits*. Columbia, 2001.


## Print


Auster, Paul. *In the Country of Last Things*. London: Faber & Faber, 1987.

Banks, Iain. *The Wasp Factory*. London: Abacus, 1990.

Benjamin, Walter. 'Theses on the Philosophy of History', in *Illuminations*, trans. Harry Zohn. New York: Schocken, pp. 253–64.

Berlin, Isaiah. *Four Essays on Liberty*. Oxford: Oxford University Press, 1969.

Caputo, John D. *Against Ethics: Contributions to a Poetics of Obligation with Constant Reference to Deconstruction*. Bloomington: Indiana University Press, 1993.

Caputo, John D. *Deconstruction in a Nutshell: A Conversation with Jacques Derrida*. New York: Fordham University Press, 1997.

Caputo, John D. *The Prayers and Tears of Jacques Derrida: Religion without Religion*. Bloomington: Indiana University Press, 1997.

Cixous, Hélène. *The Hélène Cixous Reader*, ed. Susan Sellers. London: Routledge, 1994.

Cornell, Drucilla. *The Philosophy of the Limit*. New York: Routledge, 1992.

Culler, Jonathan. *On Deconstruction: Theory and Criticism after Structuralism*. London: Routledge & Kegan Paul, 1983.

Derrida, Jacques. 'Coming into One's Own', in *Psychoanalysis and the Question of the Text*, trans. James Hulbert, ed. Geoffrey H. Hartman. Baltimore: Johns Hopkins University Press, 1978, pp. 114–48.

Derrida, Jacques. *Deconstruction Engaged: The Sydney Seminars*, ed. Paul Patton and Terry Smith. Sydney: Power Publications, 2001.

Derrida, Jacques. *Dissemination*, trans. Barbara Johnson. Chicago: University of Chicago Press, 1981.

Derrida, Jacques. *The Ear of the Other: Otobiography, Transference, Translations: Texts and Discussions with Jacques Derrida*, trans. Peggy Kamuf. New York: Schocken, 1986.

Derrida, Jacques. 'Force of Law: The "Mystical Foundation of Authority"', in *Deconstruction and the Possibility of Justice*, ed. Drucilla Cornell, Michel Rosenfeld and David Grey Carlson. London: Routledge, 1992, pp. 1–67.

Derrida, Jacques. *The Gift of Death*, trans. David Wills. Chicago: University of Chicago Press, 1995.

Derrida, Jacques. *Given Time: 1. Counterfeit Money*, trans. Peggy Kamuf. Chicago: University of Chicago Press, 1992.

Derrida, Jacques. 'Letter to a Japanese Friend', trans. David Wood and Andrew Benjamin, in *A Derrida Reader: Between the Blinds*, ed. Peggy Kamuf. New York: Columbia University Press, 1991, pp. 270–6.

Derrida, Jacques. *Limited Inc*, ed. Gerald Graff. Evanston, Ill.: Northwestern University Press, 1988.

Derrida, Jacques. *Margins of Philosophy*, trans. Alan Bass. Chicago: University of Chicago Press, 1982.

Derrida, Jacques. 'My Chances/*Mes Chances*: A Rendezvous with Some Epicurean Sterophonies', trans. Irene Harvey and Avital Ronell, in *Taking Chances: Derrida, Psychoanalysis, and Literature*, ed. Joseph H. Smith and William Kerrigan. Baltimore: Johns Hopkins University Press, 1984, pp. 1–32.

Derrida, Jacques. *Of Grammatology*, trans. Gayatri Chakravorty Spivak. Baltimore and London: Johns Hopkins University Press, 1976.

Derrida, Jacques. *Of Spirit: Heidegger and the Question*, trans. Geoffrey Bennington and Rachel Bowlby. Chicago: University of Chicago Press, 1989.

Derrida, Jacques. *On the Name*, ed. Thomas Dutoit. Stanford: Stanford University Press, 1995.

Derrida, Jacques. *The Other Heading: Reflections on Today's Europe*, trans. Pascale-Anne Brault and Michael B. Naas. Bloomington: Indiana University Press, 1992.

Derrida, Jacques. *Politics of Friendship*, trans. George Collins. London: Verso, 1997.

Derrida, Jacques. *Positions*, trans. Alan Bass. Chicago: University of Chicago Press, 1981.

Derrida, Jacques. *The Post-Card: From Socrates to Freud and Beyond*, trans. Alan Bass. Chicago: University of Chicago Press, 1987.

Derrida, Jacques. *Specters of Marx: The State of the Debt, the Work of Mourning, and the New International*, trans. Peggy Kamuf. New York and London: Routledge, 1994.

Derrida, Jacques. *Speech and Phenomena and Other Essays on Husserl's Theory of Signs*, trans. David Allison. Evanston, Ill.: Northwestern University Press, 1973.

Derrida, Jacques. *Spurs: Nietzsche's Styles*, trans. Barbara Harlow. Chicago: Chicago University Press, 1972.

Derrida, Jacques. 'The Time is Out of Joint', trans. Peggy Kamuf, in *Deconstruction is/in America*, ed. Anselm Haverkamp. New York: New York University Press, 1995, pp. 14–41.

Derrida, Jacques. *The Truth in Painting*, trans. Geoff Bennington and Ian McLeod. Chicago and London: University of Chicago Press, 1987.

Derrida, Jacques. 'Ulysses Gramophone: Hear Say Yes in Joyce', trans. Tina Kendall and Shari Benstock, in *A Derrida Reader: Between the Blinds*, ed. Peggy Kamuf. New York: Columbia University Press, 1991, pp. 571–97.

Derrida, Jacques. 'The Villanova Roundtable: A Conversation with Jacques Derrida', in John D. Caputo, *Deconstruction in a Nutshell: A Conversation with Jacques Derrida*. New York: Fordham University Press, 1997, pp. 2–28.

Derrida, Jacques. *Writing and Difference*, trans. Alan Bass. London: Routledge & Kegan Paul, 1978.

Derrida, Jacques and Bernard Stiegler. *Echographies of Television*, trans. Jennifer Bajorek. Cambridge: Polity, 2002.

Donne, John. *The Complete English Poems*. Harmondsworth: Penguin, 1975.

Dryden, John. 'Defence of the Epilogue. Or, An Essay on the Dramatique Poetry of the Last Age', in *Eighteenth-Century English Literature*, ed. Geoffrey Tillotson, Paul Fussell, Jr. and Marshall Waingrow. New York: Harcourt, Brace & World, 1969, pp. 86–92.

Editor, 'Merit in Double Jeopardy Idea', in *The West Australian*, 11 Feb. 2003, p. 12.

Forster, E. M. *Aspects of the Novel*. Harmondsworth: Penguin, 1962.

Freud, Sigmund. *Beyond the Pleasure Principle*, in *The Standard Edition of the Complete Psychological Works of Sigmund Freud*, Vol. 18, trans. James Strachey. London: Hogarth, 1986, pp. 7–64.

Freud, Sigmund. *The Interpretation of Dreams*, trans. James Strachey. Harmondsworth: Penguin, 1991.

Freud, Sigmund. *New Introductory Lectures on Psychoanalysis*, trans. James Strachey. Harmondsworth: Penguin, 1991.

Freud, Sigmund. 'A Note upon the "Mystic Writing-Pad"', in *The Standard Edition of the Complete Psychological Works of Sigmund Freud*, Vol. 19, trans. James Strachey. London: Hogarth, 1986, pp. 227–32.

Freud, Sigmund. *The Psychopathology of Everyday Life*, trans. Alan Tyson, ed. James Strachey with Angela Richards and Alan Tyson. Harmondsworth: Penguin,1960.

Fukuyama, Francis. *The End of History and the Last Man*. New York: Free Press, 1992.

Gregory, Andrew. 'Lawyers Back Double Jeopardy', *The West Australian*, 11 Feb. 2003, p. 5.

Hartley, John. *Understanding News*. London: Methuen, 1982.

Hasted, Nick. 'Apocalypse Wow!', *Uncut*, Jan. 2000, pp. 39–66.

Heidegger, Martin. *The Basic Problems of Phenomenology*, trans. A. Hofstadter. Bloomington: Indiana University Press, 1982.

Heidegger, Martin. *Being and Time*, trans. John Macquarrie and Edward Robinson. Oxford: Blackwell, 1962.

Heidegger, Martin. *Early Greek Thinking*, trans. D. F. Krell. New York: Harper & Row, 1975.

Heidegger, Martin. 'Letter on Humanism', trans. Frank Capuzzi, in *Martin Heidegger: Basic Writings*, ed. David Krell. New York: Harper & Row, 1977, pp. 193–242.

Heidegger, Martin. *Nietzsche*, Vol. 1, *The Will to Power as Art*, trans. D. F. Krell. New York: Harper & Row, 1979.

Hogg, James. *The Private Memoirs and Confessions of a Justified Singer*, ed. John Carey. Oxford: Oxford University Press, 1970.

Husserl, Edmund. *Ideas*, trans. W. R. Boyce Gibson. New York: Humanities, 1969.

Johnson, Barbara. 'Translator's Introduction', in Jacques Derrida, *Dissemination*, trans. Barbara Johnson. Chicago: University of Chicago Press, 1981, pp. vii–xxxiii.

Kant, Immanuel. 'An Answer to the Question: What is Enlightenment?', trans. H. B. Nisbet, in *Kant's Political Writings*, ed. Hans Reiss. Cambridge: Cambridge University Press, 1970, pp. 54–60.

Kant, Immanuel. *The Critique of Judgement*, trans. James Creed Meredith. Oxford: Clarendon Press, 1952.

Kant, Immanuel. *Critique of Practical Reason*, trans. Lewis White Beck. New York: Garland, 1976.

Kristeva, Julia. *Nations without Nationalism*, trans. Leon. S. Roudiez. New York: Columbia University Press, 1993.

Lacoue-Labarthe, Philippe and Jean-Luc Nancy. *The Literary Absolute: The Theory of Literature in German Romanticism*, trans. Philip Barnand and Cheryl Lester. Albany, NY: State University of New York Press, 1988.

Levinas, Emmanuel. *Totality and Infinity: An Essay on Exteriority*, trans. Alphonso Lingis. Pittsburgh: Duquesne University Press, 1969.

Lucy, Niall. *Beyond Semiotics: Text, Culture and Technology*. London: Continuum, 2001.

Lucy, Niall. *Debating Derrida*. Melbourne: Melbourne University Press, 1995.

Lucy, Niall. *Postmodern Literary Theory: An Introduction*. Oxford: Blackwell, 1997.

Lucy, Niall. 'Structuralism and the Structuralist Controversy', in *The Edinburgh Encyclopedia of Modern Criticism and Theory*, ed. Julian Wolfreys. Edinburgh: Edinburgh University Press, 2002, pp. 743–50.

Lyotard, Jean-François. *The Postmodern Condition: A Report on Knowledge*, trans. Geoff Bennington and Brian Masumi. Theory and History of Literature 10. Manchester: Manchester University Press, 1986.

Marx, Karl. 'Address to the Communist League', in *The Marxist Reader*, ed. Emile Burns. New York: Avenel, 1982, pp. 60–71.

Melville, Herman. *The Confidence-Man, His Masquerade*, ed. Hennig Cohen. New York: Holt, Rinehart & Winston, 1964.

Milton, John. 'The Readie and Easy Way to Establish a Free Commonwealth', in *Selected Prose*, ed. C. A. Patrides. Harmondsworth: Penguin, 1974, pp. 327–58.

Monk, Ray. *Ludwig Wittgenstein: The Duty of Genius*. London: Vintage, 1990.

Nietzsche, Friedrich. *On the Genealogy of Morals*, in *Basic Writings of Nietzsche*, ed. and trans. Walter Kaufmann. New York: Modern Library, 1968.

Nietzsche, Friedrich. *The Will to Power: An Attempted Transvaluation of All Values*, trans. Anthony M. Ludovici. London: George Allen & Unwin, 1924.

Norris, Christopher. *Deconstruction: Theory and Practice*. London: Methuen, 1982.

Norris, Christopher. *Derrida*. London: Fontana, 1987.

Plato. *Phaedrus*, trans. R. Hackford. Cambridge: Cambridge University Press, 1952.

Plato. *Timaeus*, trans. H. R. P. Lee. Harmondsworth: Penguin, 1965.

Rorty, Richard. 'Philosophy as a Kind of Writing', in *Consequences of Pragmatism*. Minneapolis: University of Minnesota Press, 1982, pp. 89–109.

Rousseau, Jean-Jacques. *Essay on the Origin of Languages and Writings Related to Music*, trans. and ed. John T. Scott. Hanover: University Press of New England, 1998.

Sartre, Jean Paul. *The Age of Reason*, trans. Eric Sutton. Harmondsworth: Penguin, 1986.

Saussure, Ferdinand de. *Course in General Linguisitics*, trans. Wade Baskin. London: Fontana, 1974.

Shakespeare, William. *Hamlet*, ed. John Dover Wilson. Cambridge: Cambridge University Press, 1936.

Shakespeare, William. *King Lear*, ed. Kenneth Muir. London: Methuen, 1964.

Smith, Joseph H. and William Kerrigan, 'Introduction', in *Taking Chances: Derrida, Psychoanalysis, and Literature*, ed. Smith and Kerrigan. Baltimore: Johns Hopkins University Press, 1984, pp. vii–xvi.

Spivak, Gayatri Chakravorty. 'Translator's Preface', in Jacques Derrida, *Of Grammatology*, trans. Gayatri Chakravorty Spivak. Baltimore and London: Johns Hopkins University Press, 1976, pp. ix–lxxxvii.

Thwaites, Tony. *Joycean Temporalities: Debts, Promises, and Countersignatures*. Gainesville: University Press of Florida, 2001.

Trocchi, Alexander. *Cain's Book*. New York: Grove Press, 1992.

Wark, McKenzie. 'Too Real', in *Prefiguring Cyberculture: An Intellectual History*, ed. Darren Tofts, Annemarie Jonson and Alessio Cavallaro. Sydney: Power Publications, 2002, pp. 154–64.

# Index